The Catholic Handbook for
Visiting the Sick
and Homebound

2010
Year C

LTP

LITURGY
TRAINING
PUBLICATIONS

Published with the approval of the
Committee on Divine Worship
United States Conference of Catholic Bishops.

Most "explanations of the reading" are from *Daily Prayer 2010* Liturgy Training Publications
(Chicago), 2009. The "explanations of the reading" for December 8, 2009, December 13, 2009,
December 25, 2009, February 28, 2010, March 7, 2010, March 14, 2010, March 21, 2010,
May 23, 2010, and May 30, 2010 are from *Sourcebook for Sundays, Seasons, and Weekdays:
The Almanac for Pastoral Liturgy 2010:* Liturgy Training Publications (Chicago), 2009. Those on
pages 154 and 223 are from *Daily Prayer 2007:* Liturgy Training Publications (Chicago), 2006.

Inside art by Sister Mary Grace Thul, OP

LTP appreciates your comments and suggestions. Email us at CHVS@LTP.org.

THE CATHOLIC HANDBOOK FOR VISITING THE SICK AND HOMEBOUND 2010 © 2009 Archdiocese of
Chicago: Liturgy Training Publications, 3949 North Hermitage Avenue, Chicago IL 60609;
1-800-933-1800, fax 1-800-933-7094, e-mail orders@ltp.org. All rights reserved. See our
Web site at www.LTP.org.

LTP is going green!

LTP now prints the text of *The Catholic Handbook for Visiting the Sick and Homebound 2010*
with ink that contains renewable linseed oil on paper that is 100% recycled and contains
a minimum of 40% postconsumer waste. The paper for this product was de-inked by
a process that uses PCF (Processed Chlorine Free) technologies, unlike many de-inking
processes that use toxic bleach. ✪

The printing process used to manufacture this book uses a non-heatset process that
significantly reduces emission of volatile organic compounds (VOCs) into the atmosphere.

LTP continues to work toward responsible stewardship of the environment. For more
information on our efforts, please go to www.LTP.org/environment.

Printed in the United States of America.

ISBN 978-1-56854-725-1
VS10

TABLE OF CONTENTS

INTRODUCTION

Suffering wears a thousand faces, and every face is Christ's. When we suffer sickness, loss, violence, or the harsher effects of aging in ourselves or in those we love, we cannot really understand the reasons, but we can choose the rock on which to stand. We are members of the Body of Christ. Christ our Head becomes present in our suffering; in our dying we share his death; his voyage through death to the glory of the Resurrection becomes our journey. In him, we are held securely in the face of the anxiety, fear, anger, guilt, and grief that sickness, aging, or suffering can bring.

One of the deepest causes of suffering experienced by those whom sickness or aging confines to the narrow world of home, hospital, or geriatric facility is a sense of isolation. We may feel misunderstood, rejected, abandoned by the healthy world of which we were a part, even by those who love us, even by God. There is something wrong with us. We are no longer useful. We cause other people discomfort and inconvenience. We may know how we "ought" to pray in times of suffering, but we can't seem to do it. We can't even go to church.

When we have suffered traumatic loss or violence, we may suffer a similar sense of loneliness. Our experience has set us apart. We may feel that no one can understand what we have endured. We find ourselves unable to take an interest in the world of everyday concerns about which others are busy. We may even find ourselves ill at ease with our ordinary companions in faith and worship. Our usual forms of prayer no longer seem to suffice. We have questions that are difficult to answer: Why me? Why has God allowed this to happen? We may be angry with God *and* ashamed of our anger. On the other hand, we may find ourselves more deeply in communion with the suffering Christ or with his bereaved and sorrowful Mother than before yet separated from others by the intensity of our spiritual experience.

Ministers of Care, both the laity and the ordained, are sent to step across the moat that isolates the sufferers, bringing them the comfort of personal presence and prayer. Ministries of care are as diverse as the parishes that sponsor them. Some parishes may have full-time lay pastoral associates or other employees who specialize in pastoral care. These lay people may have been specially trained, participating in pastoral care internships (Clinical Pastoral Education), or receiving undergraduate or graduate degrees in pastoral care or diocesan or national certification. Parishes also may be fortunate to have volunteers who provide pastoral care to those in hospitals, hospices, nursing homes, prisons, police stations, crisis centers, and to those who are dying or have lost a loved one. These volunteers can provide music, proclaim scripture, offer words of consolation and hope, or simply silent presence.

The most familiar ministry of care is that of Extraordinary Minister of Holy Communion. The word *extraordinary* can be confusing. In this case, the Church uses it officially to distinguish between ordained bishops, priests, and deacons, who are the *ordinary* ministers of Holy Communion, and specially commissioned lay people who fill the gaps, so to speak, when there are not enough ordinary ministers to give Holy Communion to everyone at Mass or to take Holy Communion to the sick and the homebound. The words *extraordinary* and *ordinary* as they are used here may seem odd because they recall a time when there were so many priests that there was no need for lay people to take on this role.

This handbook is specially designed for the use of *lay* Ministers of Care, so it does *not* contain the rites for the sacraments of Penance or the Anointing of the Sick, or the special prayers and blessings used by ordained bishops, priests, or deacons. All lay ministers who provide care to those who are sick, homebound, isolated, or suffering in some way will benefit from the contents of this book.

You, as a Minister of Care, have been called to be a sign and a bridge. Sent by the parish, you are the living witness that the community of faith and worship has not forgotten the absent sick, the invisible elderly, and the unseen sufferers. Praying with them as a representative of Christ living in the Church, you are a sign that God is and wants to be with them. You draw them back into conscious communion with the whole Body of Christ. They, and in many cases their caregivers, are not alone.

The Church has provided two official books which contain a wealth of rites for those who visit, pray with, or bring Holy Communion to the sick, aging, dying, or others who are struggling with addiction, personal violence, or the loss of a child through miscarriage—especially those cut off from fully participating in the liturgical life of their local Church or parish. These ritual books are called *Pastoral Care of the Sick: Rites of Anointing and Viaticum* and the *Book of Blessings*. *Pastoral Care of the Sick* contains rites specific to those who are sick and dying, providing orders of prayer for the sacraments of Eucharist, Penance, and Anointing of the Sick. The *Book of Blessings* provides multiple orders of blessing for various needs and occasions. What you have in your hand, *The Catholic Handbook for Visiting the Sick and Homebound 2010*, is a booklet containing all of the rituals from *Pastoral Care of the Sick* and the *Book of Blessings* that can be used by lay people when visiting the sick and the homebound. Everything you will need is right here! You will be able to use this book when you are sent to give Holy Communion to other parishioners or pray with: those who are confined to their homes, to hospitals, or to geriatric centers; those who have suffered the traumatic loss of a child through miscarriage; those who suffer from addictions; and those who have been victims of violence. The most important resource you have as a minister, though, is your personal relationship with Christ, our healer and our Savior. You too are the face of Christ.

USING THIS BOOK

The Catholic Handbook for Visiting the Sick and Homebound 2010 will tell you what the Church asks of you, as her spokesperson, to say and do when you visit, pray with, or give Holy Communion to those who suffer. You need not worry about making up prayers—they are provided here for you! In fact, *except* where the rite itself calls for adaptation, you must use the prayers as they are written because they express the common faith of the Catholic Church to which we all committed ourselves in Baptism.

CONTENTS OF THIS BOOK

You, as a Minister of Care, will be called upon to offer those whom you visit an opportunity to benefit from the strengthening power of prayer by making use of one many rites and orders of prayer and blessing provided by the Church. This book contains everything you will need to give Holy Communion and other rites for praying with the sick and others who suffer for various reasons. The rites and prayers are divided into three sections:

- Section 1: Blessings of and Visits to the Sick and Suffering (pages 20–77)

- Section 2: Holy Communion (pages 78–93)

- Section 3: Pastoral Care of the Dying (pages 94–136)

Each of these sections contains the official rites and orders of prayer as provided by the Church in both the *Book of Blessings* and *Pastoral Care of the Sick: Rites of Anointing and Viaticum.*

BLESSINGS OF AND VISITS TO THE SICK AND SUFFERING

Visiting and Blessing the Sick: You may be sent to visit the sick simply to pray with them. However, sometimes you may be prepared to give Holy Communion, but you discover that those you are visiting are unable to receive for some reason. At still other times, you may be visiting Catholic patients in an institution, but others who are not Catholic recognize you as a minister and ask you to pray with them. You need not turn away, feeling that you have nothing to offer. These are just a few of the situations when you could use these rites for visiting the sick and the suffering—either to prepare them to receive Holy Communion during a later visit or simply to enable them to draw strength and comfort from the healing presence of Christ.

Titles of these rites: Some clarification about the titles of the services contained in this book is needed to prevent confusion. The book entitled *Pastoral Care of the Sick: Rites of Anointing and Viaticum* provides two rites for visiting the sick: "Visits to the Sick" and "Visits to a Sick Child." "Visits to the Sick" is used with adults. The *Book of Blessings* also provides two rites. These two rites are entitled "Order for the Blessing of Adults" and "Order for the Blessing of Children." Here the word "order" simply means "order of service." These two "orders" presents an entire service of optional song, scripture, prayer, and blessing. The two rites from *Pastoral Care of the Sick* are simple prayers for visiting the sick.

The Liturgies: The "Orders for the Blessing of the Sick" (see pages 20–32) begin with a simple sign of the cross and invitation to pray followed by a reading of the Word of God whereas "Visits to the Sick" (see pages 64–72) begin with the reading. "Visits to the Sick" continues with the Lord's Prayer and a choice of concluding prayers designed to address some of the different circumstances in which the sick might find themselves. For example, concluding prayer option A references those who "suffer pain, illness or disease"; option B pleas for the sick to be restored to health; and option C requests that the sick may find "peace of mind." Consider your options in relation to the situation of the person you are visiting. If you happen to be visiting someone who isn't Catholic, you may use this order of service, but remember to remind them tactfully that Catholics end the Lord's Prayer after "deliver us from evil." If not, be prepared for them to add the longer ending, "for thine is the kingdom, the power and the glory" before the "Amen." Above all, you do not want to cause distress to anyone.

In the "Orders for Blessing of the Sick" the Word of God may be followed with an explanation of the reading then a litany of intercession. The Church urges the minister to encourage the sick to participate in Christ's redemptive work by uniting their sufferings to his and by praying for the needs of the world. Prayer for others is an effective antidote to the self-preoccupation to which sickness and aging can tempt us. Intercessions provide an excellent way of meeting this need. You may allow participants the opportunity to add petitions of their own, but beware of causing embarrassment by prolonging the silence if it becomes clear that they have nothing to say.

Both the rites for "Visits to the Sick" and "Orders for the Blessing of the Sick" end with prayers of blessing which may be said over the person who is ill. The "Orders for the Blessing of the Sick" provides two prayers of blessing. The first option is for more than one person, whereas the second option is for a single individual. The rite stipulates that the minister is to make the sign of the cross on the forehead of the sick while saying the prayer. The gesture may be unexpected or unfamiliar, especially coming from a lay minister, so it is wise to let people know what you are preparing to do. This may be followed with a prayer for the protection of the Blessed Virgin Mary. The rite suggests singing a familiar Marian song. If music is unavailable, only sing if those you are visiting are able to participate.

"Orders for the Blessing of the Sick" and "Visits to the Sick" end with a concluding prayer. In both rites, the "lay minister invokes the Lord's blessing on the sick and all present by signing himself or herself with the sign of the cross."

"Visits to the Sick" includes two prayers of blessing: one for a sick person and one for the elderly. Please note that the lay minister does not make the same gesture as given in "Orders for the Blessing of the Sick." Simply say the prayer.

The "Order for the Blessing of Children" (page 29) and "Visits to a Sick Child" (page 73) follow the same pattern as those used for adults, but they use simpler language. You will have to decide which rite or order of blessing is appropriate to use with older children. A word of caution: Before you make the sign of the cross on the child's head during the blessing, it would be wise to alert parents or caregivers to see if they have any objections. It is also wise to explain this to the child. Remember that very sick children may have experienced unpleasant medical procedures and may fear the unexplained touch of an unfamiliar adult.

Visiting and Blessing those who Suffer: The *Catholic Handbook* contains three additional services for blessing those who suffer and may not be able to participate in Sunday Eucharist:

- Blessing a Person Suffering from Addiction or from Substance Abuse

- Blessing a Victim of Crime or Oppression

- Blessing Parents after a Miscarriage

You may meet people in need of one of these special blessings. You may meet them in a health care setting. For example, a patient may have been hospitalized as a result of addictive behavior or alcohol and drug abuse. Sometimes you may meet a patient who has suffered personal violence, such as domestic abuse, rape, a drive-by shooting, injuries sustained in an accident caused by a drunk driver, injuries sustained at the hands of those engaged in criminal activities, such as robbery, or a person afflicted from post-traumatic stress disorder. You may also find that a woman has suffered a miscarriage, and she and the father are grieving together. You may also find people among the families of those you are visiting to pray with them or give them Holy Communion at home or in an institutional environment. An elderly person might indicate a child or grandchild who is suffering one of these needs and ask you to pray with them. You may be among those assigned to special ministries of care in settings such as support groups.

Be aware that the reason for the need may be recent or long-standing. Sometimes, someone who is coping with illness, confinement in a geriatric facility, or other situation which has brought you to them will want to discuss something that happened long ago and continues to haunt them. Periods of inactivity brought on by sickness or aging give us plenty of time to think and may spur us to make peace with the past in a new way. These orders of blessing offer that opportunity.

Whenever you meet someone in one of these situations, you may use the appropriate order of blessing from the pages that follow. All of them follow the same pattern: an opening rite (sign of the cross, simple greeting, optional introduction), reading and response, including the opportunity to comment on the reading, intercessions, the Lord's Prayer, a prayer of blessing directed to the particular needs of participants, and a concluding rite (general blessing). The Church encourages adaptation, provided the order of service is followed and the major elements included. For example, you might want to personalize the opening introduction, following the general pattern of the one provided here. Here is one example of a personalized introduction to the "Order for Blessing a Victim of Crime or Oppression." Imagine that you are praying with and for a young woman who is a victim of date rape. You might say something like this: *"God has always shown care and compassion for people who have suffered acts of violence, like the one that has brought you here. We commend you, [use the woman's name], to God, who binds up all our wounds, heals us from the pain of betrayal, and restores us to our rightful dignity as a child of God."* The introduction now refers to the victim's own experience, uses her name, and avoids language that could summon up frightening images of being held by a male person.

You will want to choose those intercessions that are most appropriate. You may invite participants to add their own and you may also do so. Turning one's own suffering into prayer for others is both a way of uniting oneself with the redemptive suffering of Christ and turning one's attention outward. If you are accustomed to using the "Orders for Blessing of the Sick," please note that there are some differences between them and these orders of blessing for those otherwise in distress. In particular, these latter orders call for the Lord's Prayer, which often provides the comfort of a familiar prayer; and they do *not* call for the minister to touch the person while saying the prayer of blessing for them. This can be an important courtesy when using this order for blessing with those who have suffered personal violence and shy away from being touched by strangers, even in prayers of blessing.

Like the "Orders for the Blessing of the Sick," these orders also provide a shorter form: a short invitation to prayer, a short reading, and a prayer of blessing. These short forms are particularly useful when ministering to those who have very recently experienced a crisis in addiction, an incident of violence, or a miscarriage, and are too distressed to concentrate on a longer ritual. They are also helpful when you are visiting the person for some other reason and find a need to help them deal with one of these issues.

One of the hidden benefits of the Church's rites of prayer is that they teach us to think in harmony with the Church. If you have never experienced the particular need for which you are blessing someone, your good intentions may sometimes stumble in trying to find the right words of comfort. It is easy to offend without meaning to by offering what sound like platitudes to those who are in the immediate throes of suffering. It is also easy to give impressions of God that hurt rather than help them. The texts of these rites will assist you to reflect on how to focus your comments. They are also impersonal enough that they offer room for participants in the rites to take them as words from God to be pondered and applied to their own experience rather than as personal remarks about their own faith response to what they have suffered.

HOLY COMMUNION

This book provides two rites for lay ministers to give Holy Communion to the sick: "Communion in Ordinary Circumstances" and "Communion in a Hospital or Institution."

Communion in Ordinary Circumstances: The first form, called "Communion in Ordinary Circumstances," is especially useful if you are taking Holy Communion to the sick or aging in their homes. It assumes two things: First, that you have enough time to lead the full rite of Holy Communion including a short Liturgy of the Word; second, that those you visit are well enough to participate in a full service. The Church urges us always to consider the needs of the sick or aging. If they are very weak or tire quickly, it's better to shorten or omit elements like the explanation after the reading or the General Intercessions (Prayer of the Faithful), or simply to use the shorter form called "Communion in a Hospital or Institution" even in a home setting.

Communion in a Hospital or Institution: This second form, "Communion in a Hospital or Institution," provides a minimal format mainly intended for use when you are visiting many patients individually in an institutional setting. The Church expresses a strong preference for avoiding this abbreviated format even in an institution. Instead, it is suggested that, if possible, you gather several residents together in one or more areas and celebrate the full rite of "Communion in Ordinary Circumstances." If that is not possible, the Church recommends that you add elements from the fuller rite, such as the reading of the word, unless participants are too weak. On the other hand, in the case of extremely sick people, you may shorten "Communion in a Hospital or Institution" by omitting as much of the rite as necessary. Try to include at least a greeting, the Lord's Prayer, the customary responses that precede Holy Communion itself, and the closing prayer.

PASTORAL CARE OF THE DYING

Viaticum: Holy Communion for the Dying: Any of the seriously ill, but especially hospice patients, may move more quickly than expected toward death. A person who faces death within days should receive Holy Communion under the form of Viaticum. "Viaticum" means something like "travel with you," but it is often translated as food for the journey. Although the sacrament of Anointing of the Sick strengthens us in the face of sickness, Eucharist as Viaticum is the sacrament that, together with Penance, prepares a person for the final journey through death to everlasting life in Christ. Catholics are obligated to receive Viaticum if possible. The sacrament of Anointing of the Sick may be given after Penance but *before* Viaticum. If the person is unable to swallow, they may receive the Sacrament of Penance *instead* of Viaticum; however, the Church teaches that Viaticum is the essential sacrament when we are in the face of death. The time for using the special comforting and strengthening prayers of the Rite of Viaticum to administer Holy Communion is while the person is still conscious and able to swallow. Once death has become imminent, dying persons may receive Viaticum every day for as long as they are able. An Extraordinary Minister of Holy Communion may and should give Viaticum to the dying. If the dying person has not received sacramental absolution, please make sure the person has the opportunity for both the Sacrament of Penance and, if desired, Anointing of the Sick.

Commendation for the Dying and Prayers for the Dead: While the sacraments, especially Viaticum, unite the dying with Christ in his passage from this life to the next, we also gather with the dying and those around them to sustain this union through the prayer and faith of the Church.

"Commendation for the Dying" does not follow a fixed pattern. You may select any texts from the prayers, litanies, aspirations, psalms and readings, or you may use other familiar prayers, such as the rosary. If you have had the opportunity to talk with the dying person and loved ones or others present, choose texts you think will sustain and strengthen them according to their spiritual needs and other circumstances. Pray the texts slowly and quietly, allowing ample opportunities for silence. You may repeat them as often as needed, especially prayers that have special meaning for those present. Even those who are unconscious and dying can sometimes hear more than we realize. If the dying cannot hear, loved ones present will find comfort in the prayers.

If you minister in an institutional setting, you may find that those who are not Catholic will ask you to pray with and for them. You may use these texts with and for any who are in need of the consolation of prayer. The texts drawn from the Bible are especially likely to bring comfort.

Once death has occurred, you will find both prayers for the dead and prayers for family and friends on page 132, "Prayers for the Dying."

Ritual Preparation: All of the rites are simple to follow. Look them over before making your visits in order to familiarize yourself with the order of prayer. Directions are included and parts are clearly marked so that you can easily lead the assembly in prayer.

THE GOSPEL FOR SUNDAYS AND HOLY DAYS OF OBLIGATION

Following the rites is the Gospel for Sundays and holy days of obligation for Year C. Remember the Church has a three year cycle of readings. In 2011 the readings will be from Year A. The Church recommends reading the week's Sunday Gospel during the rites for Holy Communion as one important way of uniting the communicants in spirit with the parish from which sickness or age has separated them.

In this book, the Gospel is clearly labeled by date and the title of particular observances so that you can easily find the appropriate reading. For example, if you make your visit during the Second Week of Lent, you will use the Gospel for the Second Sunday of Lent. In 2010, this Sunday of Lent is February 28. Simply look for the date and the title of the celebration and you will know which Gospel to use. For some observances, such as Palm Sunday, the Lectionary provides a longer and shorter form of the Gospel. For simplicity, only the shorter form is included in this resource.

If you are visiting on a holy day of obligation, use the Gospel prescribed for these days. You can also locate the Gospel for holy days of obligation by date and title. In the dioceses of the United States of America, the holy days of obligation occurring in 2010 are:

- Solemnity of the Immaculate Conception of the Blessed Virgin Mary (December 8, 2009)

- Solemnity of the Nativity of the Lord (December 25, 2009)

- Solemnity of the Blessed Virgin Mary, the Mother of God (January 1, 2010)

- Solemnity of the Ascension of the Lord (May 13 or May 16, 2010)

- Solemnity of All Saints (November 1, 2010)

Please also note that the solemnity of the Assumption of the Blessed Virgin Mary (August 15) falls on a Sunday—remember, all Sundays are obligatory.

If you are visiting very young sick children, you might want to obtain a copy of the appropriate reading from the *Lectionary for Masses with Children* from your parish. Another option is to read the Gospel passages recommended in "Visits to a Sick Child."

If you are praying with those who are struggling with addictions, the aftermath of violence, or with parents who have suffered the loss of a child through miscarriage, you will usually find the readings recommended in the orders of blessing more appropriate to their circumstances than the Gospel for the Sunday. However, if appropriate, feel free to use the Gospel for Sundays and holy days of obligation. To discern which readings to use, it is best to look over the order of service *before* the visit occurs.

EXPLANATION OF THE READINGS

You will notice that the rites offer an opportunity for the Minister of Care to give a brief explanation of the reading with special reference to the experience of those with whom you are praying and, where appropriate, of their caregivers. If you are using the Sunday or holy day reading, you might want to base your explanation and reflection on the parish Sunday homily in order to deepen the sense of connection you are trying encourage. If you feel uncomfortable about speaking, you will find a brief explanation of the reading after the Gospel for each Sunday and holy day. If you choose to read it from the book, it would be a good idea to ponder it and make it your own so that the words come from your heart and not merely from the page. The Word of God itself creates a bond between reader and hearers, breaking down the sense of isolation that afflicts sufferers. Explanatory words that are spoken, or even read, with sincerity and personal conviction will support this pastoral relationship more effectively than words read mechanically.

PATRON SAINTS

Finally, there is a list of saints who the Church has identified as particular intercessors, companions, and guides for those suffering various kinds of afflictions, whether physical or emotional. If you feel that those with whom you pray would welcome the company and support of a saint, you might want to include the saint's name in the intercessions (petitions) and suggest that those you are visiting continue to ask for the saint's help. An example of an intercession is: *For all those who suffer from throat cancer, especially N. (insert the name of the person or persons present), that through the intercession of Saint Blaise, may find comfort and strength, we pray to the Lord.*

This book does not provide any information about the saints listed, but there are many books and Web sites where you can find their stories. Such resources are *Butler's Lives of the Saints* (published by the Liturgical Press), Catholic Online, (www.catholic.org/saints), and the Catholic Forum (http://www.catholic-forum.com/saints/).

BEYOND THE BOOK

The official rites offer appropriate prayers and clear directions, but they don't tell you everything you need to know in order to lead the rituals effectively. Here are some practical hints that may help.

GETTING FROM THE PARISH CHURCH TO YOUR PASTORAL ASSIGNMENT

Scheduling a Visit: Some parishes assign ministers to visit particular people but encourage them to make their own arrangements regarding the day and time. Both those in need of your ministry and their families or caregivers, at home or in institutional facilities, appreciate being able to negotiate appropriate times for a pastoral visit or Holy Communion. It gives them an opportunity to make sure that they and those they would like to have present can be there. For example, if you're visiting the sick, you don't want to drop in when patients are absent from their rooms for tests or treatments.

If you are asked to take Holy Communion to the sick and the homebound at times other than during Sunday Mass, please make sure your training includes information about where to find the tabernacle key and how to approach the tabernacle reverently, open it, and transfer the hosts you will need from the ciborium in which they are kept to the container you will use to carry the Blessed Sacrament to the sick (see below). It is particularly important to arrange with the parish coordinator a convenient time for you to obtain the tabernacle key, because it is not permitted to keep the Eucharist at home or carry it all day as you go about your ordinary business before visiting communicants.

Ordinarily, when taking the Blessed Sacrament from the tabernacle, you would pray briefly before the tabernacle, wash your fingers in a small vessel of water that is usually kept beside the tabernacle for that purpose, wipe them on a finger towel also usually kept there, and genuflect after opening the tabernacle. If your parish does not provide either the small vessel or finger towel, wash your hands in the sacristy or otherwise clean your fingers as best you are able over the sacrarium (a sink flowing directly into the ground for water from purifications, from the first washings of the altar cloths, or the water containing the completely dissolved consecrated hosts which cannot be properly consumed).

If you have unused hosts left over at the end of your rounds, you must bring them back to the parish church and replace them in the tabernacle. After closing the tabernacle, you again wash your fingers. You may also cleanse the empty pyx (a dignified vessel, often round, used to carry the consecrated host) in the sacarium if it appears to contain crumbs. Fill it with water, drink the water, and dry the pyx carefully on a finger towel, if available.

If you wish to avoid having hosts that must be returned, you can give the last few communicants more than one host so that all the hosts are consumed or consume them yourself as part of the Communion rite during your last visit, provided all the usual requirements for Holy Communion are met. However, you may not simply consume them yourself after your last visit because Holy Communion is always received in the context of public prayer rather than simply as a matter of convenience by the minister alone. Similarly, you may not take the remaining hosts home to return later to the Church because the Eucharist must be kept in a tabernacle or other designated locked place of reservation in a church.

Bringing What You Need: Make a checklist of what you want to have with you before you leave home. You'll find some suggestions below. Don't forget this book! It does happen. If it does, don't panic, and don't fail to keep your appointment. As a precaution, make every effort to memorize the outline of the rites you expect to use or keep a copy of a simple outline in your pocket, wallet, or purse. In this case, do make up your own prayer, but keep it very short and simple. Borrow a Bible or summarize the Gospel in your own words. God works through all our weaknesses and mistakes.

Carrying the Blessed Sacrament: The Blessed Sacrament is in the pyx or in another dignified vessel reserved exclusively for that purpose. Your parish will probably supply you with what you need. Some pyxes can be worn or carried in a pouch on a cord around the neck. When you are carrying the Blessed Sacrament, remember and attend reverently to Christ, choosing your activities appropriately, without becoming artificially silent or stilted in your conversation, especially with those who are not aware of what you are carrying or of its significance. On the one hand, avoid distractions such as loud music, "talk" programs or other television shows, movies or DVDs/tapes, or other things that would disturb prayer while you are en route. On the other hand, while avoiding such distractions, be careful not to be rude to people who greet you or speak to you in passing as you walk to your destination. Christ is not offended by the company and conversation of human beings! You should make your Communion visit immediately upon leaving the Church.

Music Preparation: Sometimes it might be possible to incorporate music into your visits. Music most certainly can be included in the rites and orders of blessing. Singing familiar melodies and texts can be extremely comforting and healing to those who are suffering. Hospitals, nursing homes, and other facilities might have a piano or you might bring a guitar. A capella singing can be just as effective. Be sure to select music in which either the refrain is simple or are familiar melodies, and that the texts give a message of Christ's hope. Here are some suggestions: *Blest Are They; Jesus, Heal Us; Healer of Our*

Every Ill; Lord of All Hopefulness; I Heard the Voice of Jesus Say; Remember Your Love; Shepherd Me, O God; You Are Mine.

PREPARING AN ENVIRONMENT FOR PRAYER

ENCOUNTERING CHRIST IN PERSONS

Church ministry is always personal. It is important that you spend a few minutes at the beginning of your visit to get to know those present and give them a chance to feel comfortable with you. Your parish may be able to supply you with helpful information in advance of your visit. In return, it would be useful to other Ministers of Care if you were to report back what you had learned about the condition, circumstances, and needs of those you visit.

When you arrive, put those present at ease by engaging in a few moments of personal conversation. Tell them your name and remind them that the parish has sent you. Ask how they are and listen attentively to their answers. If you are visiting the sick, show your interest and concern, but remember that you are not there to offer medical advice or to pass judgment on medical matters, even if you yourself are a professional medical caregiver. If you can, address those you are visiting by name, but be aware that not everyone likes to be addressed by a first name without permission. Sickness, debilitating aging, and other forms of public suffering often rob people of their sense of personal dignity, so treating people with respect is an important dimension of your ministry. Whatever their condition, you and they are both collaborators in Christ's work. Ministry is a two-way street: those whom you visit are serving you by their witness to Christ suffering as much as you are serving them by offering them Christ's loving comfort. Take note of any special needs you see: is the sufferer low on energy, in pain, limited in motion, hard of hearing, angry, sad, or seemingly depressed? You will want to tailor the length, content, and style of the celebration accordingly.

PREPARING YOURSELF TO LEAD PRAYER

The world of the suffering, especially those confined to home or, even more so, to a hospital or geriatric facility may not feel much like a place of prayer. The most important element in creating an environment for prayer is you. The minister who prays while leading others in prayer is the most powerful invitation one can offer to those who need to be called from all the preoccupations of suffering into deeper awareness of the mystery of God present and acting in our midst.

Here are some steps you can take to develop this important skill:

1) Devote time for praying, reading, and meditating on the texts of the prayers and readings provided in this book. You will best pray them in public if you have already prayed them many times in private.

2) Familiarize yourself thoroughly with the structure and flow of the rites so that you can concentrate on the people rather than the book. You need not memorize prayers or readings. Simply know what comes next and where to find it.

3) Before you go into the building or room, pray briefly, asking Christ to work through you; after the visit, pause to give thanks.

4) Reflect on your experience after you return home. Were there moments during the celebration when you felt uncertain or distracted? Why? What could you do next time to make yourself more at ease so that you can pray more attentively without losing contact with those you are leading in prayer? Sharing experience with other Ministers of Care or parish staff can be a useful way to continue and deepen everyone's continuing ministry formation.

Preparing the Room for Prayer

You can also take some simple steps to establish an atmosphere that encourages prayer when circumstances allow. A small standing crucifix, cross, or icon heightens consciousness of Christ. Appropriate lighting can help, where possible. In an institutional setting, for example, a lamp or sunlight creates a more calming environment than do fluorescent lights. If you are taking Holy Communion to someone, take a small white cloth and a candle with you to prepare a place on which to put the pyx containing the Blessed Sacrament as a focus for the celebration as you lead the other prayers. (Be sure you have something with which to light the candle!) A corporal (traditionally a square white, linen cloth upon which is placed sacred vessels holding the Blessed Sacrament) is not required, but if it is used, it is traditionally placed on top of another white cloth rather than on a bare surface. Caregivers familiar with the rite may have prepared a place in advance, but many will not.

Be aware of the restrictions you may face in a health care or geriatric facility. The rites for Holy Communion recommends that the minister be accompanied by a candle-bearer and place a candle on the table where the Blessed Sacrament will stand during the celebration, as described above. However, safety regulations usually forbid the use of open flames in institutions. Oxygen and other substances that might be in use are highly flammable. Moreover, you may not be able to find any appropriate surface other than a bedside table or night stand that will have to be cleared before you can set up a place for the Blessed Sacrament. Be prepared to make whatever practical adjustments the circumstances require. If you have never visited a particular hospital unit or nursing home, see if you can find another minister who has and find out what to expect.

PREPARING PARTICIPANTS FOR PRAYER

After a few moments of conversation, find a graceful way to end the social part of the visit without seeming uninterested or abrupt. Then give the participants a simple, brief overview of the rite you will be using so they will know what to expect, unless you know they are already familiar with the rite. Surprises tend to disrupt prayer! It's especially important to decide in advance who will do the reading. The directions say that the reading may be done "by one of those present or by the minister." If you don't know the participants, the best solution might be to ask for a volunteer (and allow the volunteer a few moments to prepare), but remember that not everyone is willing or able to read in public with short notice, especially in times of distress. Finally, mark the beginning of prayer clearly by inviting silent attentiveness, making the sign of the cross and moving into the service itself.

RECOGNIZING THE RECIPIENT

You are ministering not only to those to whom the ritual is addressed but also to those around them, whether loved ones or caregivers. Be sure to include them by looking and speaking to them, as well as to the person who is your focus. When you are saying prayers of blessing over the sufferer, your attention is on that person alone, but all present are invited to join in the "Amen" that affirms and concludes the prayer. Practice with another minister until you can say prayers in such a way that others know when and how to respond without having a book in front of them.

WHO MAY RECEIVE HOLY COMMUNION

Catholic shut-ins, caregivers, or others who assemble with them may receive Holy Communion provided the usual conditions have been met. You can offer that invitation before you begin the rite for Holy Communion, being careful not to embarrass or offend those who are not eligible to receive. "The elderly, the infirm and those who care for them can receive the Holy Eucharist even if they have eaten something within the preceding hour" (Code of Canon Law, 919 §2).

SPECIAL CIRCUMSTANCES

Unfortunately, neither sickness nor the deterioration sometimes brought on by aging is neat or predictable. The physical, psychological, and spiritual condition of those you visit may have changed since the arrangements for your visit were made. You may need to make unprepared changes in the rite or blessing you are using to meet the current need.

Special Circumstances for Extraordinary Ministers of Holy Communion: If you are taking Holy Communion to the sick or elderly, sometimes those you are visiting will express reluctance to receive. They may or may not want to tell you why. They might be embarrassed to say that they are too nauseated; they might feel alienated from God; they might need sacramental absolution but don't want to say so. You are obviously a person of generosity and compassion, or you wouldn't have volunteered to be an Extraordinary Minister of Holy Communion. However, a Holy Communion visit is not ordinarily the best time to identify and try to resolve serious personal or spiritual problems. Be aware of your status and of the vulnerability of the suffering: you represent the Church, and you have more power than you may realize to make others feel guilty by showing that you disapprove of their decision not to receive Holy Communion or by giving the impression that they have wasted your time. Remember that they are not rejecting you as a person. Rather, they are struggling with something deeper. Offer to pray with them, using the rites provided for visiting or blessing the sick. Invite them to enter more deeply into communion with the suffering and risen Christ who loves them. Let them know what pastoral resources are available to them: offer to return or to send another minister at a more convenient time; provide the parish phone number; offer to let the pastoral staff know that they would like a priest to visit, without forcing them to reply. If the parish distributes a bulletin during the weekend Masses, bring one along to leave with the person to whom you are visiting.

Sometimes you may find that those you are visiting are unable to swallow easily. Consult medical caregivers. If they give permission, you may break the host into the smallest of pieces, place a piece on the person's tongue to dissolve, and follow with a glass of water to make swallowing possible. Be careful with crumbs when you break the host. The best thing to do is to break the host carefully over the pyx so that crumbs will fall into the pyx. If any crumbs fall on the cloth or table on which the pyx has been placed, moisten your finger, pick up all the crumbs very carefully, and consume them reverently.

You may even find that someone cannot ingest the host at all. In such cases, the person may receive the Blood of Christ, but that requires specialized vessels and procedures. Report the circumstances to your pastor, parish coordinator, or to the facility chaplain's office if the person is in a health care or geriatric facility. They will be able to appropriately give Holy Communion. In the meantime, use one of the rites for visiting or blessing the sick to give them the support of your presence and prayer.

Be aware that the hospitalized may not be permitted to take anything by mouth for a period of time prior to certain tests or treatments. Even a small piece of the host received at such times may cause medical personnel to cancel the planned procedure. If you see a sign that says "Nothing by mouth" or "NPO," initials for the Latin phrase *nil per os*, meaning the same thing, ask a member of the medical staff if you may administer Holy Communion, but expect a "no." In this case, too, you should still pray with the sick or aging, using one of the rites for visiting or blessing the sick. Remember that you still offer them the comfort of Christ's presence in his word and through your own presence and that of the parish you represent.

Don't be alarmed by moments of silence. Sometimes ministers think they need to fill silences with conversation or action. There is nothing wrong with sitting in silence with another. In fact, these can be quite healing moments. God is present in these moments.

You should also be cognizant of those who are either not able to speak, have difficulty speaking, or speak rather slowly. Be patient and allow them to respond as they are able.

It is important that the Extraordinary Minister of Holy Communion keeps in mind the sacramental rites which are an essential part of the Church's ministry to the sick and dying and which can be administered *only* by an ordained bishop or priest—the sacraments of Penance (Reconciliation) and the Anointing of the Sick. As appropriate, it is part of your ministry to bring these to the attention of the sick and those confined to their homes, and if needed, to help them contact a priest.

SERVICE TO THE PEOPLE OF GOD

Among these nuts and bolts of the ministry of care, never lose sight of your purpose. You have been commissioned in the name of Christ and his Church to serve as a bridge builder across the isolation that separates the sick and suffering from the parish community of faith and worship. Your deepest task is to carry the Good News of the Gospel to those who stand in need of its healing power. With your parish or diocesan training program, the support of your parish pastoral staff and other Ministers of Care, this book and your growing experience, you have many of the tools you will need. However, the most important tool is one that only Christ can provide for you. The more deeply you yourself enter into the heart of the Gospel message, the more clearly you will see that sick and healthy, young and old, grieving and rejoicing, struggling and at peace, are all one Body. In that Body, we are *all* servants of the Good News we proclaim, building one another up in faith and love until that day when, by God's gracious gift, we will all dwell together in the Lord's own house for ever and ever.

Genevieve Glen, OSB
Abbey of Saint Walburga
Virginia Dale CO
Revised January 2007

About the Author:

Sister Genevieve Glen, OSB, is a Benedictine nun of the contemplative Abbey of St. Walburga in Virginia Dale, CO. She holds master's degrees in systematic theology from Saint John's University, Collegeville, Minnesota, and in spirituality from the Catholic University of America in Washington DC, where she also did extensive doctoral studies in liturgy. She has lectured and written extensively on the Church's rites for the sick and dying. She is co-author of the *Handbook for Ministers of Care,* second edition (Liturgy Training Publications) and contributing editor of *Recovering the Riches of Anointing: A Study of the Sacrament of the Sick* (The Liturgical Press).

THE RITES

Orders for the Blessing of the Sick

INTRODUCTION

376 The blessing of the sick by the ministers of the Church is a very ancient custom, having its origins in the practice of Christ himself and his apostles. When ministers visit those who are sick, they are to respect the provisions of *Pastoral Care of the Sick: Rites of Anointing and Viaticum*, nos. 42–56, but the primary concern of every minister should be to show the sick how much Christ and his Church are concerned for them.

377 The text of *Pastoral Care of the Sick* indicates many occasions for blessing the sick and provides the blessing for formularies.[13]

378 The present order may be used by a priest or deacon. It may also be used by a layperson, who follows the rites and prayers designated for a lay minister. While maintaining the structure and chief elements of the rite, the minister should adapt the celebration to the circumstances of the place and the people involved.

379 When just one sick person is to be blessed, a priest or deacon may use the short formulary given in no. 406.

---

13. See Roman Ritual, *Pastoral Care of the Sick: Rites of Anointing and Viaticum*, no. 54.

ORDER OF BLESSING

A. ORDER FOR THE BLESSING OF ADULTS
INTRODUCTORY RITES

380   *When the community has gathered, the minister says:*

In the name of the Father, and of the Son, and of the Holy Spirit.

All make the sign of the cross and reply:

Amen.

382   *A lay minister greets those present in the following words.*

Brothers and sisters, let us bless the Lord, who went about doing good and healing the sick. Blessed be God now and for ever.
R. *Blessed be God now and for ever.*

Or:

R. *Amen.*

383   *In the following or similar words, the minister prepares the sick and all present for the blessing.*

The Lord Jesus, who went about doing good works and healing sickness and infirmity of every kind, commanded his disciples to care for the sick, to pray for them, and to lay hands on them. In this celebration we shall entrust our sick brothers and sisters to the care of the Lord, asking that he will enable them to bear their pain and suffering in the knowledge that, if they accept their share in the pain

of his own passion, they will also share in its power
to give comfort and strength.

READING OF THE WORD OF GOD

384   *A reader, another person present, or the minister reads a text of sacred
Scripture, taken preferably from the texts given in* Pastoral Care of the Sick *and
the* Lectionary for Mass.[14] *The readings chosen should be those that best apply to
the physical and spiritual condition of those who are sick.*

**Brothers and Sisters, listen to the words of the second
letter of Paul to the Corinthians:**   1:3–7

The God of all consolation.

Blessed be the God and Father of our Lord Jesus
Christ, the Father of compassion and God of all
encouragement, who encourages us in our every
affliction, so that we may be able to encourage those
who are in any affliction with the encouragement
with which we ourselves are encouraged by God. For
as Christ's sufferings overflow to us, so through
Christ does our encouragement also overflow. If we
are afflicted, it is for your encouragement and
salvation; if we are encouraged, it is for your
encouragement, which enables you to endure the
same sufferings that we suffer. Our hope for you is
firm, for we know that as you share in the sufferings,
you also share in the encouragement.

---

14. See ibid, no. 297; Lectionary for Mass (2nd ed., 1981), nos. 790–795, 796–
     800 (Ritual Masses: V. Pastoral Care of the Sick and the Dying, 1. Anointing
     of the Sick and 2. Viaticum), and nos. 933–937 (Masses for Various Needs
     and Occasions, III. For Various Public Needs, 24. For the Sick).

385   Or:

**Brothers and sisters, listen to the words of the
holy gospel according to Matthew:**   11:28–30

Come to me and I will refresh you.

Jesus said to the crowds: "Come to me, all you who
labor and are burdened, and I will give you rest. Take
my yoke upon you and learn from me, for I am meek
and humble of heart; and you will find rest for yourselves. For my yoke is easy, and my burden light."

386   Or:

**Brothers and sisters, listen to the words of the holy
gospel according to Mark:**   6:53–56

They laid the sick in the marketplace.

After making the crossing, Jesus and his disciples
came to land at Gennesaret and tied up there. As
they were leaving the boat, people immediately
recognized him. They scurried about the surrounding
country and began to bring in the sick on mats to
wherever they heard he was. Whatever villages or
towns or countryside he entered, they laid the sick in
the marketplaces and begged him that they might
touch only the tassel on his cloak; and as many as
touched it were healed.

*387   As circumstances suggest, one of the following responsorial psalms may
be sung or said, or some other suitable song.*

R. *Lord, you have preserved my life from destruction.*

Isaiah 38

Once I said,
"In the noontime of life I must depart!
To the gates of the nether world I shall
be consigned
for the rest of my years." *R.*

I said, "I shall see the LORD no more
in the land of the living.
No longer shall I behold my fellow men
among those who dwell in the world." *R.*

My dwelling, like a shepherd's tent,
is struck down and borne away from me;
You have folded up my life, like a weaver
who severs the last thread. *R.*

Those live whom the LORD protects;
yours . . . the life of my spirit.
You have given me health and life. *R.*

Psalm 102:2–3, 24–25
*R. (v. 2) O Lord, hear my prayer, and let my cry come
to you.*

388   *As circumstances suggest, the minister may give those present a brief
explanation of the biblical text, so that they may understand through faith the
meaning of the celebration.*

INTERCESSIONS

389   The intercessions are then said. The minister introduces them and an assisting minister or one of those present announces the intentions. From the following intentions those best suited to the occasion may be used or adapted, or other intentions that apply to those who are sick and to the particular circumstances may be composed.

The minister says:

The Lord Jesus loves our brothers and sisters who are ill. With trust let us pray to him that he will comfort them with his grace, saying:
R. *Lord, give those who are sick the comfort of your presence.*

Assisting minister:

Lord Jesus, you came as healer of body and of spirit, in order to cure all our ills. R.

Assisting minister:

You were a man of suffering, but it was our infirmities that you bore, our sufferings that you endured. R.

Assisting minister:

You chose to be like us in all things, in order to assure us of your compassion. R.

Assisting minister:

You experienced the weakness of the flesh in order to deliver us from evil. R.

Assisting minister:

At the foot of the cross your Mother stood as companion in your sufferings, and in your tender care you gave her to us as our Mother. R.

Assisting minister:

It is your wish that in our own flesh we should fill up what is wanting in your sufferings for the sake of your Body, the Church. **R.**

390   *Instead of the intercessions or in addition to them, one of the following litanies taken from* Pastoral Care of the Sick, *nos. 245 and 138 may be used.*

Minister:

You bore our weakness and carried our sorrows: Lord, have mercy.
R. *Lord, have mercy.*

Minister:

You felt compassion for the crowd, and went about doing good and healing the sick: Christ, have mercy.
R. *Christ, have mercy.*

Minister:

You commanded your apostles to lay their hands on the sick in your name: Lord, have mercy.
R. *Lord, have mercy.*

391   *Or:*

The minister says:

Let us pray to God for our brothers and sisters and for all those who devote themselves to caring for them.

Assisting minister:

Bless **N.** and **N.** and fill them with new hope and strength: Lord, have mercy.
R. *Lord, have mercy.*

Relieve their pain: Lord, have mercy. **R.**

Free them from sin and do not let them give way to temptation: Lord, have mercy. **R.**

Assisting minister:

Sustain all the sick with your power: Lord, have mercy. **R.**

Assisting minister:

Assist all who care for the sick: Lord, have mercy. **R.**

Assisting minister:

Give life and health to our brothers and sisters on whom we lay our hands in your name: Lord, have mercy. **R.**

PRAYER OF BLESSING

394   *A lay minister traces the sign of the cross on the forehead of each sick person and says the following prayer of blessing.*

Lord, our God,
who watch over your creatures with unfailing care,
keep us in the safe embrace of your love.
With your strong right hand raise up your servants
        (**N.** and **N.**)
and give them the strength of your own power.

Minister to them and heal their illnesses,
so that they may have from you the help they
   long for.

We ask this through Christ our Lord.
R. Amen.

395   Or, for one sick person:
Lord and Father, almighty and eternal God,
by your blessing you give us strength and support
   in our frailty:
turn with kindness toward this your servant N.
Free him/her from all illness and restore him/her
   to health,
so that in the sure knowledge of your goodness
he/she will gratefully bless your holy name.

We ask this through Christ our Lord.
R. Amen.

396   After the prayer of blessing the minister invites all present to pray
for the protection of the Blessed Virgin. They may do so by singing or reciting
a Marian antiphon, for example, We turn to you for protection (Sub tuum
praesidium) or Hail, Holy Queen.

CONCLUDING RITE

398   A lay minister invokes the Lord's blessing on the sick and all present by
signing himself or herself with the sign of the cross and saying:
May the Lord Jesus Christ,
who went about doing good and healing the sick,

grant that we may have good health
and be enriched by his blessings.
R. Amen.

B. ORDER FOR THE BLESSING OF CHILDREN

*399   For the blessing of sick children, the texts already given are to be adapted
to the children's level, but special intercessions are provided here and a special
prayer of blessing.*

INTERCESSIONS

*400   To the following intentions others may be added that apply to the
condition of the sick children and to the particular circumstances.*

The minister says:

The Lord Jesus loved and cherished the little ones
with a special love. Let us, then, pray to him for these
sick children, saying:
R. *Lord, keep them in all their ways.*

Or:

R. *Lord, hear our prayer.*

Assisting minister:

Lord Jesus, you called the little children to come to
you and said that the kingdom of heaven belongs to
such as these; listen with mercy to our prayers for
these children. (For this we pray:) *R.*

Assisting minister:

You revealed the mysteries of the kingdom of heaven,
not to the wise of this world, but to little children;

give these children the proof of your love. (For this
we pray:) *R.*

Assisting minister:

You praised the children who cried out their
Hosannas on the eve of your passion; strengthen
these children and their parents with your holy
comfort. (For this we pray:) *R.*

Assisting minister:

You charged your disciples to take care of the sick;
stand at the side of all those who so gladly devote
themselves to restoring the health of these children.
(For this we pray:) *R.*

PRAYER OF BLESSING

402   *A lay minister, and particularly a mother or father when blessing a sick
child, traces the sign of the cross on each child's forehead and then says the
following prayer of blessing.*

Father of mercy and God of all consolation,
you show tender care for all your creatures
and give health of soul and body.
Raise up these children
        (*or* this child *or* the son/daughter you have
        given us)
        from their (his/her) sickness.
Then, growing in wisdom and grace in your sight
        and ours,
they (he/she) will serve you all the days of their
        (his/her) life

in uprightness and holiness
and offer the thanksgiving due to your mercy.

We ask this through Christ our Lord.
R. Amen.

C. SHORTER RITE

403   *The minister says:*
Our help is in the name of the Lord.

All reply:
Who made heaven and earth.

404   *One of those present or the minister reads a text of sacred Scripture, for example:*

2 Corinthians 1:3–4
Blessed be the God and Father of our Lord Jesus Christ, the Father of compassion and God of all encouragement, who encourages us in our every affliction, so that we may be able to encourage those who are in any affliction with the encouragement with which we ourselves are encouraged by God.

Matthew 11:28–29
Jesus said, "Come to me, all you who labor and are burdened, and I will give you rest. Take my yoke upon you and learn from me, for I am meek and humble of heart; and you will find rest for yourselves."

405 *As circumstances suggest . . . a lay minister may trace the sign of the cross on the sick person's forehead while saying the prayer.*

Lord and Father, almighty and eternal God,
by your blessing you give us strength and support in
   our frailty:
turn with kindness toward your servant, N.
Free him/her from all illness and restore him/her
   to health,
so that in the sure knowledge of your goodness
he/she will gratefully bless your holy name.

We ask this through Christ our Lord.
R. Amen.

Order for the Blessing of a Person Suffering from Addiction or from Substance Abuse

INTRODUCTION

407   Addiction to alcohol, drugs, and other controlled substances causes great disruption in the life of an individual and his or her family. This blessing is intended to strengthen the addicted person in the struggle to overcome addiction and also to assist his or her family and friends.

408   This blessing may also be used for individuals who, although not addicted, abuse alcohol or drugs and wish the assistance of God's blessing in their struggle.

409   Ministers should be aware of the spiritual needs of a person suffering from addiction or substance abuse, and to this end the pastoral guidance on the care of the sick and rites of *Pastoral Care of the Sick* will be helpful.

410   If the recovery process is slow or is marked by relapses, the blessing may be repeated when pastorally appropriate.

411   These orders may be used by a priest or a deacon, and also by a lay person, who follows the rites and prayers designated for a lay minister.

A. ORDER OF BLESSING

INTRODUCTORY RITES

412   *When the community has gathered, a suitable song may be sung. After the singing the minister says:*

In the name of the Father, and of the Son, and of the Holy Spirit.

All make the sign of the cross and reply:

Amen.

414   *A lay minister greets those present in the following words:*

Let us praise God our creator, who gives us courage and strength, now and for ever.

R. Amen.

415   *In the following or similar words, the minister prepares those present for the blessing.*

God created the world and all things in it and entrusted them into our hands that we might use them for our good and for the building up of the Church and human society. Today we pray for N., that God may strengthen him/her in his/her weakness and restore him/her to the freedom of God's children. We pray also for ourselves that we may encourage and support him/her in the days ahead.

READING OF THE WORD OF GOD

416   A reader, another person present, or the minister reads a text of
sacred Scripture.

**Brothers and sisters, listen to the words of the second
letter of Paul to the Corinthians:** 4:6–9

We are afflicted, but not crushed.

For God who said, "Let light shine out of darkness,"
has shone in our hearts to bring to light the knowledge of the glory of God on the face of Jesus Christ.

But we hold this treasure in earthen vessels, that the
surpassing power may be of God and not from us.
We are afflicted in every way, but not constrained;
perplexed, but not driven to despair; persecuted, but
not abandoned; struck down, but not destroyed.

417   Or:

Isaiah 63:7–9—He has favored us according to his mercy.

*Romans 8:18–25—I consider the sufferings of the present to be as nothing
compared with the glory to be revealed in us.*

Matthew 15:21–28—Woman, you have great faith.

418   *As circumstances suggest, one of the following responsorial psalms may
be sung or said, or some other suitable song.*

R. *Our help is from the Lord who made heaven and earth.*

Psalm 121

I lift up my eyes toward the mountains;
whence shall help come to me?

My help is from the LORD
who made heaven and earth. **R.**

May he not suffer your foot to slip;
may he slumber not who guards you:
Indeed he neither slumbers nor sleeps,
the guardian of Israel. **R.**

The LORD is your guardian; the LORD is your shade;
he is beside you at your right hand.
The sun shall not harm you by day,
nor the moon by night. **R.**

The LORD will guard you from all evil;
he will guard your life.
The LORD will guard your coming and your going,
both now and forever. **R.**

Psalm 130:1–2, 3–4, 5–6, 7–8
R. *(v. 5) My soul trusts in the Lord.*

419   *As circumstances suggest, the minister may give those present a brief explanation of the biblical text, so that they may understand through faith the meaning of the celebration.*

INTERCESSIONS

420   *The intercessions are then said. The minister introduces them and an assisting minister or one of those present announces the intentions. From the following those best suited to the occasion may be used or adapted, or other intentions that apply to the particular circumstances may be composed.*

The minister says:

Our God gives us life and constantly calls us to new life; let us pray to God with confidence.
R. *Lord, hear our prayer.*

Assisting minister:

For those addicted to alcohol/drugs, that God may be their strength and support, we pray. **R.**

Assisting minister:

For **N.**, bound by the chains of addiction/substance abuse, that we encourage and assist him/her in his/her struggle, we pray. **R.**

Assisting minister:

For **N.**, that he/she may trust in the mercy of God through whom all things are possible, we pray. **R.**

Assisting minister:

For the family and friends of **N.**, that with faith and patience they show him/her their love, we pray. **R.**

Assisting minister:

For the Church, that it may always be attentive to those in need, we pray. **R.**

421   *After the intercessions the minister, in the following or similar words, invites all present to sing or say the Lord's Prayer.*

Let us pray to our merciful God as Jesus taught us:

All:

Our Father . . .

PRAYER OF BLESSING

422   *A lay minister says the prayer with hands joined.*

A   *For addiction*

God of mercy,
we bless you in the name of your Son, Jesus Christ,
who ministered to all who came to him.
Give your strength to N., your servant,
bound by the chains of addiction.
Enfold him/her in your love
and restore him/her to the freedom of God's children.

Lord,
look with compassion on all those
who have lost their health and freedom.
Restore to them the assurance of your
        unfailing mercy,
and strengthen them in the work of recovery.

To those who care for them,
grant patient understanding and a love
        that perseveres.

We ask this through Christ our Lord.
R. Amen.

B   *For substance abuse*

God of mercy,
we bless you in the name of your Son, Jesus Christ,

who ministered to all who came to him.
Give your strength to *N.*, your servant,
enfold him/her in your love
and restore him/her to the freedom of God's children.

Lord,
look with compassion on all those
who have lost their health and freedom.
Restore to them the assurance of your
            unfailing mercy,
strengthen them in the work of recovery,
and help them to resist all temptation.

To those who care for them,
grant patient understanding and a love
            that perseveres.

We ask this through Christ our Lord.
R. Amen.

As circumstances suggest, the minister in silence may sprinkle the person with holy water.

CONCLUDING RITE

424   *A lay minister concludes the rite by signing himself or herself with the sign of the cross and saying:*

May our all-merciful God, Father, Son, and Holy Spirit, bless us and embrace us in love for ever.
R. Amen.

425   *It is preferable to end the celebration with a suitable song.*

B. SHORTER RITE

426   *All make the sign of the cross as the minister says:*

Our help is in the name of the Lord.

All reply:

Who made heaven and earth.

427   *One of those present or the minister reads a text of sacred Scripture, for example:*

Brothers and sisters, listen to the words of the second letter of Paul to the Corinthians: 4:6–9

We are afflicted, but not crushed.

For God who said, "Let light shine out of darkness," has shone in our hearts to bring to light the knowledge of the glory of God on the face of Jesus Christ.

But we hold this treasure in earthen vessels, that the surpassing power may be of God and not from us. We are afflicted in every way, but not constrained; perplexed, but not driven to despair; persecuted, but not abandoned; struck down, but not destroyed.

428   *Or:*

Isaiah 63:7–9—He has favored us according to his mercy.

Matthew 15:21–28—Woman, you have great faith.

429   *A lay minister says the prayer with hands joined.*

A   *For addiction*
God of mercy,
we bless you in the name of your Son, Jesus Christ,
who ministered to all who came to him.
Give your strength to **N.**, your servant,
bound by the chains of addiction.
Enfold him/her in your love
and restore him/her to the freedom of God's children.

Lord,
look with compassion on all those
who have lost their health and freedom.
Restore to them the assurance of your
        unfailing mercy,
and strengthen them in the work of your recovery.

To those who care for them,
grant patient understanding and a love
        that perseveres.

We ask this through Christ our Lord.
R. Amen.

B *For substance abuse.*

God of mercy,
we bless you in the name of your Son, Jesus Christ,
who ministered to all who came to him.
Give your strength to **N.**, your servant,
enfold him/her in your love
and restore him/her to the freedom of God's children.

Lord,
look with compassion on all those
who have lost their health and freedom.
Restore to them the assurance of your
    unfailing mercy,
strengthen them in the work of recovery,
and help them to resist all temptation.

To those who care for them,
grant patient understanding and a love
    that perseveres.

We ask this through Christ our Lord.
R. Amen.

Order for the Blessing of a Victim of Crime or Oppression

INTRODUCTION

430   The personal experience of a crime, political oppression, or social oppression can be traumatic and not easily forgotten. A victim often needs the assistance of others, and no less that of God, in dealing with this experience.

431   This blessing is intended to assist the victim and help him or her come to a state of tranquility and peace.

432   These orders may be used by a priest or a deacon, and also by a layperson, who follows the rites and prayers designated for a lay minister.

A. ORDER OF BLESSING

INTRODUCTORY RITES

433   When the community has gathered, a suitable song may be sung. After the singing, the minister says:

In the name of the Father, and of the Son, and of the Holy Spirit.

All make the sign of the cross and reply:

Amen.

435   A lay minister greets those present in the following words:

May the Lord grant us peace, now and for ever.
R. Amen.

436   In the following or similar words, the minister prepares those present for the blessing.

Throughout history God has manifested his love and care for those who have suffered from violence, hatred, and oppression. We commend **N.** to the healing mercy of God who binds up all our wounds and enfolds us in his gentle care.

READING OF THE WORD OF GOD

437   A reader, another person present, or the minister reads a text of sacred Scripture.

Brothers and sisters, listen to the words of the holy gospel according to Matthew: 10:28–33

Do not fear.

Jesus said to his disciples: "Do not be afraid of those who kill the body but cannot kill the soul; rather, be afraid of the one who can destroy both soul and body in Gehenna. Are not two sparrows sold for a small coin? Yet not one of them falls to the ground without your Father's knowledge. Even all the hairs of your head are counted. So do not be afraid; you are worth more than many sparrows. Everyone who acknowledges me before others I will acknowledge before my heavenly Father. But whoever denies me before others, I will deny before my heavenly Father."

438   Or:

Isaiah 59:6b–8, 15–18—The Lord is appalled by evil and injustice.

Job 3:1–26—Lamentation of Job.

Lamentations 3:1–24—I am one who knows affliction.

Lamentations 3:49–59—When I called, you came to my aid.

Micah 4:1–4—Every person shall sit undisturbed.

Matthew 5:1–10—The beatitudes.

Matthew 5:43–48—Love your enemies, pray for those who persecute you.

Luke 10:25–37—The good Samaritan.

439   As circumstances suggest, one of the following responsorial psalms may be sung, or some other suitable song.

R. *The Lord is my strength and my salvation.*

Psalm 140

Deliver me, O LORD, from evil men;
preserve me from violent men,
From those who devise evil in their hearts,
and stir up wars ever day. *R.*

Save me, O LORD, from the hands of the wicked;
preserve me from violent men
Who plan to trip up my feet—
the proud who have hidden a trap for me;
They have spread cords for a net;
by the wayside they have laid snares for me. *R.*

Grant not, O LORD, the desires of the wicked;
further not their plans.
Those who surround me lift up their heads;
may the mischief which they threaten
　　　　overwhelm them. *R.*

I know that the LORD renders
justice to the afflicted, judgment to the poor.
Surely the just shall give thanks to your name;
the upright shall dwell in your presence. *R.*

Psalm 142:2–3, 4b–5, 6–7
R. (v. 6) You, O Lord, are my refuge.

Psalm 31:2–3a, 4–5, 15–16, 24–25
R. (v. 6) Into your hands I commend my spirit.

440　As circumstances suggest, the minister may give those present a brief
*explanation of the biblical text, so that they may understand through faith the
meaning of the celebration.*

INTERCESSIONS

441　*The intercessions are then said. The minister introduces them and an
assisting minister or one of those present announces the intentions. From the*

following those best suited to the occasion may be used or adapted, or other intentions that apply to the particular circumstances may be composed.

The minister says:

Let us pray to the Lord God, the defender of the weak and powerless, who delivered our ancestors from harm.

R. *Deliver us from evil, O Lord.*

Assisting minister:

For **N.**, that he/she may be freed from pain and fear, we pray to the Lord. R.

Assisting minister:

For all who are victims of crime/oppression, we pray to the Lord. R.

Assisting minister:

For an end to all acts of violence and hatred, we pray to the Lord. R.

Assisting minister:

For those who harm others, that they may change their lives and turn to God, we pray to the Lord. R.

442   *After the intercessions the minister, in the following or similar words, invites all present to sing or say the Lord's Prayer.*

The Lord heals our wounds and strengthens us in our weakness; let us pray as Christ has taught us:

All:

Our Father . . .

PRAYER OF BLESSING

443   A lay minister says the prayer with hands joined.

Lord God,

your own Son was delivered into the hands of
        the wicked,

yet he prayed for his persecutors

and overcame hatred with the blood of the cross.

Relieve the suffering of N.;

grant him/her peace of mind

and a renewed faith in your protection and care.

Protect us all from the violence of others,

keep us safe from the weapons of hate,

and restore to us tranquility and peace.

We ask this through Christ our Lord.

R. Amen.

*As circumstances suggest, the minister in silence may sprinkle the person with
holy water.*

CONCLUDING RITE

*445   A lay minister concludes the rite by signing himself or herself with the
sing of the cross and saying:*

May God bless us with his mercy,

strengthen us with his love,

and enable us to walk in charity and peace.

R. Amen.

446   It is preferable to end the celebration with a suitable song.

SHORTER RITE

447 *All make the sign of the cross as the minister says:*

Our help is in the name of the Lord.

All reply:

Who made heaven and earth.

448 *One of those present or the minister reads a text of sacred Scripture, for example:*

Brothers and sisters, listen to the words of the holy gospel according to Matthew: 10:28–33

Do not fear.

Jesus said to his disciples: "Do not be afraid of those who kill the body but cannot kill the soul; rather, be afraid of the one who can destroy both soul and body in Gehenna. Are not two sparrows sold for a small coin? Yet not one of them falls to the ground without your Father's knowledge. Even all the hairs of your head are counted. So do not be afraid; you are worth more than many sparrows. Everyone who acknowledges me before others I will acknowledge before my heavenly Father. But whoever denies me before others, I will deny before my heavenly Father."

449 *Or:*

Isaiah 59:6b–8, 15–18—The Lord is appalled by evil and injustice.

Job 3:1–26—Lamentation of Job.

Lamentations 3:1–24—I am a man who knows affliction.

Lamentations 3:49–59—When I called, you came to my aid.

Matthew 5:1–10—The beatitudes.

Luke 10:25–37—The good Samaritan.

450   *A lay minister says the prayer with hands joined.*

Lord God,

your own Son was delivered into the hands of
        the wicked

yet he prayed for his persecutors

and overcame hatred with the blood of the cross.

Relive the suffering of N.;

grant him/her peace of mind

and a renewed faith in your protection and care.

Protect us all from the violence of others,

keep us safe from the weapons of hate,

and restore to us tranquility and peace.

We ask this through Christ our Lord.

R. *Amen.*

Order for the Blessing of Parents after a Miscarriage

INTRODUCTION

279   In times of death and grief the Christian turns to the Lord for consolation and strength. This is especially true when a child dies before birth. This blessing is provided to assist the parents in their grief and console them with the blessing of God.

280   The minister should be attentive to the needs of the parents and other family members and to this end the introduction to the *Order of Christian Funerals*, Part II: Funeral Rites for Children will be helpful.

281   These orders may be used by a priest or deacon, and also by a layperson who follows the rites and prayers designated for a lay minister.

A. ORDER OF BLESSING

INTRODUCTORY RITES

282   *When the community has gathered, a suitable song may be sung. The minister says:*

In the name of the Father, and of the Son, and of the Holy Spirit.

All make the sign of the cross and reply:

Amen.

284   *A lay minister greets those present in the following words:*

Let us praise the Father of mercies, the God of all consolation. Blessed be God for ever.

R. *Blessed be God for ever.*

285   *In the following or similar words, the minister prepares those present for the blessing.*

For those who trust in God,
in the pain of sorrow there is consolation,
in the face of despair there is hope,
in the midst of death there is life.
N. and N., as we mourn the death of your child we place ourselves in the hands of God and ask for strength, for healing, and for love.

READING OF THE WORD OF GOD

286   *A reader, another person present, or the minister reads a text of sacred Scripture.*

**Brothers and sisters, listen to the words of the book of
Lamentations:** 3:17–26

Hope in the Lord.

My soul is deprived of peace,
I have forgotten what happiness is;
I tell myself my future is lost,
all that I hoped for from the Lord.
The thought of my homeless poverty
is wormwood and gall;
Remembering it over and over
leaves my soul downcast within me.
But I will call this to mind,
as my reason to have hope:
The favors of the LORD are not exhausted,
his mercies are not spent;
They are renewed each morning,
so great is his faithfulness.
My portion is the LORD, says my soul;
therefore will I hope in him.
Good is the LORD to one who waits for him,
to the soul that seeks him;
It is good to hope in silence
for the saving help of the LORD.

287   *Or:*

*Isaiah 49:8–13—In a time of favor I answer you, on the day of salvation
I help you.*

Romans 8:18–27—In hope we were saved.

Romans 8:26–31—If God is for us, who can be against us?

Colossians 1:9–12—We have been praying for you unceasingly.

Hebrews 5:7–10—Christ intercedes for us.

Luke 22:39–46—Agony in the garden.

288   *As circumstances suggest, one of the following responsorial psalms may be sung, or some other suitable song.*

R. *To you, O Lord, I lift up my soul.*

Psalm 25

Your ways, O LORD, make known to me;
teach me your paths,
Guide me in your truth and teach me,
for you are God my savior,
and for you I wait all the day. **R.**

Remember that your compassion, O LORD,
and your kindness are from of old.
The sins of my youth and my frailties remember not;
in your kindness remember me
because of your goodness, O LORD. **R.**

Look toward me, and have pity on me,
for I am alone and afflicted.
Relieve the troubles of my heart,
and bring me out of my distress. **R.**

Preserve my life, and rescue me;
let me not be put to shame, for I take refuge in you.
Let integrity and uprightness preserve me,
because I wait for you, O LORD. **R.**

Psalm 143:1, 5–6, 8, 30
R. *(v. 1) O Lord, hear my prayer.*

289   *As circumstances suggest, the minister may give those present a brief explanation of the biblical text, so that they may understand through faith the meaning of the celebration.*

INTERCESSIONS

290   *The intercessions are then said. The minister introduces them and an assisting minister or one of those present announces the intentions. From the following those best suited to the occasion may be used or adapted, or other intentions that apply to the particular circumstances may be composed.*

The minister says:

Let us pray to God who throughout the ages has heard the cries of parents.
R. *Lord, hear our prayer.*

Assisting minister:

For N. and N., who know the pain of grief, that they may be comforted, we pray. R.

Assisting minister:

For this family, that it may find new hope in the midst of suffering, we pray. R.

Assisting minister:

For these parents, that they may learn from the example of Mary, who grieved by the cross of her Son, we pray. R.

Assisting minister:

For all who have suffered the loss of a child, that Christ may be their support, we pray. R.

Let us pray to the God of consolation and hope, as
Christ has taught us:

All:

Our Father . . .

PRAYER OF BLESSING

292   *A minister who is a priest or deacon says the prayer of blessing with hands*
outstretched over the parents; a lay minister says the prayer with hands joined.

Compassionate God,
soothe the hearts of N. and N.,
and grant that through the prayers of Mary,
who grieved by the cross of her Son,
you may enlighten their faith,
give hope to their hearts,
and peace to their lives.

Lord,
grant mercy to all the members of this family
and comfort them with the hope
that one day we will all live with you,
with your Son Jesus Christ, and the Holy Spirit,
for ever and ever.
R. *Amen.*

293   *Or:*

Lord,
God of all creation
we bless and thank you for your tender care.

Receive this life you created in love
and comfort your faithful people in their time of loss
with the assurance of your unfailing mercy.

We ask this through Christ our Lord.
R. Amen.

As circumstances suggest, the minister in silence may sprinkle the parents with holy water.

CONCLUDING RITE

295   A lay minister concludes the rite by signing himself or herself with the sing of the cross and saying:

May God give us peace in our sorrow,
consolation in our grief,
and strength to accept his will in all things.
R. Amen.

296   It is preferable to end the celebration with a suitable song.

SHORTER RITE

297   All make the sign of the cross as the minister says:

Our help is in the name of the Lord.

All reply:

Who made heaven and earth.

**Brothers and sisters, listen to the words of the book
of Lamentations:** 3:17–26

Hope in the Lord.

My soul is deprived of peace,
I have forgotten what happiness is;
I tell myself my future is lost,
all that I hoped for from the LORD.
The thought of my homeless poverty
is wormwood and gall;
Remembering it over and over
leaves my soul downcast within me.
But I will call this to mind,
as my reason to have hope:
The favors of the LORD are not exhausted,
his mercies are not spent;
They are renewed each morning,
so great is his faithfulness.
My portion is the LORD, says my soul;
therefore will I hope in him.
Good is the LORD to one who waits for him,
to the soul that seeks him;
It is good to hope in silence
for the saving help of the LORD.

299 *Or:*

Romans 8:26–31 —If God is for us, who can be against us?

Colossians 1:9–12—We have been praying for you unceasingly.

300   *A lay minister says the prayer with hands joined.*

Compassionate God,
soothe the hearts of *N.* and *N.*,
and grant that through the prayers of Mary,
who grieved by the cross of her Son,
you may enlighten their faith,
give hope to their hearts,
and peace to their lives.

Lord,
grant mercy to all the members of this family
and comfort them with the hope
that one day we will all live with you,
with your Son Jesus Christ, and the Holy Spirit,
for ever and ever.
R. Amen.

301   *Or:*

Lord,
God of all creation,
we bless and thank you for your tender care.
Receive this life you created in love
and comfort your faithful people in their time of loss
with the assurance of your unfailing mercy.

We ask this through Christ our Lord.
R. Amen.

Pastoral Care of the Sick

INTRODUCTION

Lord, your friend is sick.

42   The rites in Part I of *Pastoral Care of the Sick: Rites of Anointing and Viaticum* are used by the Church to comfort the sick in time of anxiety, to encourage them to fight against illness, and perhaps to restore them to health. These rites are distinct from those in the second part of this book, which are provided to comfort and strengthen a Christian in the passage from this life.

43   The concern that Christ showed for the bodily and spiritual welfare of those who are ill is continued by the Church in its ministry to the sick. This ministry is the common responsibility of all Christians, who should visit the sick, remember them in prayer, and celebrate the sacraments with them. The family and friends of the sick, doctors and others who care for them, and priests with pastoral responsibilities have a particular share in this ministry of comfort. Through words of encouragement and faith they can help the sick to unite themselves with the sufferings of Christ for the good of God's people.

Remembrance of the sick is especially appropriate at common worship on the Lord's Day, during the general intercessions at Mass and in the intercessions at Morning Prayer and Evening Prayer. Family members and those who are dedicated to the care of the sick should be remembered on these occasions as well.

44 Priests have the special task of preparing the sick to celebrate the sacrament of penance (individually or in a communal celebration), to receive the eucharist frequently if their condition permits, and to celebrate the sacrament of anointing at the appropriate time. During this preparation it will be especially helpful if the sick person, the priest, and the family become accustomed to praying together. The priest should provide leadership to those who assist him in the care of the sick, especially deacons and other ministers of the eucharist.

The words "priest," "deacon," and "minister" are used advisedly. Only in those rites which must be celebrated by a priest is the word "priest" used in the rubrics (that is, the sacrament of penance, the sacrament of the anointing of the sick, the celebration of viaticum within Mass). Whenever it is clear that, in the absence of a priest, a deacon may preside at a particular rite, the words "priest or deacon" are used in the rubrics. Whenever another minister is permitted to celebrate a rite in the absence of a priest or deacon, the word "minister" is used in the rubrics, even though in many cases the rite will be celebrated by a priest or deacon.

45 The pastoral care of the sick should be suited to the nature and length of the illness. An illness of short duration in which the full recovery of health is a possibility requires a more intensive ministry, whereas illness of a longer duration which may be a prelude to death requires a more extensive ministry. An awareness of the attitudes and emotional states which these different situations engender in the sick is indispensable to the development of an appropriate ministry.

VISITS TO THE SICK

46 Those who visit the sick should help them to pray, sharing with them the word of God proclaimed in the assembly from

which their sickness has separated them. As the occasion permits, prayer drawn from the psalms or from other prayers or litanies may be added to the word of God. Care should be taken to prepare for a future visit during which the sick will receive the eucharist.

VISITS TO A SICK CHILD

47   What has already been said about visiting the sick and praying with them (see no. 46) applies also in visits to a sick child. Every effort should be made to know the child and to accommodate the care in keeping with the age and comprehension of the child. In these circumstances the minister should also be particularly concerned to help the child's family.

48   If it is appropriate, the priest may discuss with the parents the possibility of preparing and celebrating with the child the sacraments of initiation (baptism, confirmation, eucharist). The priest may baptize and confirm the child (see *Rite of Confirmation*, no. 7b). To complete the process of initiation, the child should also receive first communion. (If the child is a proper subject for confirmation, then he or she may receive first communion in accordance with the practice of the Church.) There is no reason to delay this, especially if the illness is likely to be a long one.

49   Throughout the illness the minister should ensure that the child receives communion frequently, making whatever adaptations seem necessary in the rite for communion of the sick (Chapter III).

50   The child is to be anointed if he or she has sufficient use of reason to be strengthened by the sacrament of anointing. The rites provided (Chapter IV) are to be used and adapted.

COMMUNION OF THE SICK

51   Because the sick are prevented from celebrating the eucharist with the rest of the community, the most important visits are those during which they receive holy communion. In receiving the body and blood of Christ, the sick are united sacramentally to the Lord and are reunited with the eucharistic community from which illness has separated them.

ANOINTING OF THE SICK

52   The priest should be especially concerned for those whose health has been seriously impaired by illness or old age. He will offer them a new sign of hope: the laying on of hands and the anointing of the sick accompanied by the prayer of faith (James 5:14). Those who receive this sacrament in the faith of the Church will find it a true sign of comfort and support in time of trial. It will work to overcome the sickness, if this is God's will.

53   Some types of mental sickness are now classified as serious. Those who are judged to have a serious mental illness and who would be strengthened by the sacrament may be anointed (see no. 5). The anointing may be repeated in accordance with the conditions for other kinds of serious illness (see no. 9).

Visits to the Sick

INTRODUCTION

I was sick, and you visited me.

54   The prayers contained in this chapter follow the common pattern of reading, response, prayer, and blessing. This pattern is provided as an example of what can be done and may be adapted as necessary. The minister may wish to invite those present to prepare for the reading from Scripture, perhaps by a brief introduction or through a moment of silence. The laying on of hands may be added by the priest, if appropriate, after the blessing is given.

55   The sick should be encouraged to pray when they are alone or with their families, friends, or those who care for them. Their prayer should be drawn primarily from Scripture. The sick person and others may help to plan the celebration, for example, by choosing the prayers and readings. Those making these choices should keep in mind the condition of the sick person.

    The passages found in this chapter and those included in Part III speak of the mystery of human suffering in the words, works, and life of Christ. Occasionally, for example, on the Lord's Day, the sick may feel more involved in the worship of the community from which they are separated if the readings used are those assigned for that day in the lectionary. Prayers may also be drawn from the psalms or from other prayers or litanies. The sick should be helped in making this form of prayer, and the minister should always be ready to pray with them.

56   The minister should encourage the sick person to offer his or her sufferings in union with Christ and to join in prayer for the Church and the world. Some examples of particular intentions which may be suggested to the sick person are: for peace in the world; for a deepening of the life of the Spirit in the local Church; for the pope and the bishops; for people suffering in a particular disaster.

VISITS TO THE SICK

READING

57   *The word of God is proclaimed by one of those present or by the minister.*
An appropriate reading from Part III or one of the following readings may
be used:

A   *Acts of the Apostles 3:1–10*

In the name of Jesus and the power of his Church, there is salvation—
even liberation from sickness.

B   *Matthew 8:14–17*

Jesus fulfills the prophetic figure of the servant of God taking upon himself and
relieving the sufferings of God's people.

RESPONSE

58   *A brief period of silence may be observed after the reading of the word*
of God. An appropriate psalm from Part III or one of the following psalms may
be used:

A   *Psalm 102*

R. *O Lord, hear my prayer and*
let my cry come to you.

O LORD, hear my prayer,
          and let my cry come to you.

Hide not your face from me
    in the day of my distress.
Incline your ear to me;
    in the day when I call, answer me speedily.

*R. O Lord, hear my prayer and
let my cry come to you.*

He has broken down my strength in the way;
    he has cut short my days.
        I say: O my God,
Take me not hence in the midst of my days;
    through all generations your years endure.

*R. O Lord, hear my prayer and
let my cry come to you.*

Of old you established the earth,
    and the heavens are the work of your hands.
They shall perish, but you remain
    though all of them grow old like a garment.
Like clothing you change them, and they are changed,
    but you are the same,
and your years have no end.

*R. O Lord, hear my prayer and
let my cry come to you.*

Let this be written for the generation to come,
    and let his future creatures praise the LORD:

"The LORD looked down from his holy height,
 from heaven he beheld the earth,
To hear the groaning of the prisoners,
 to release those doomed to die."

R. *O Lord, hear my prayer and*
let my cry come to you.

B *Psalm 27*

R. *The Lord is my light and my salvation.*

The LORD is my light and my salvation;
 whom should I fear?
The LORD is my life's refuge;
 of whom should I be afraid?

R. *The Lord is my light and my salvation.*

One thing I ask of the LORD;
 this I seek:
To dwell in the house of the LORD
 all the days of my life
That I may gaze on the loveliness of the LORD
 and contemplate his temple.

R. *The Lord is my light and my salvation.*

For he will hide me in his abode
 in the day of trouble,

He will conceal me in the shelter of his tent,
 he will set me high upon a rock.

R. *The Lord is my light and my salvation.*

*The minister may then give a brief explanation of the reading, applying it to the
needs of the sick person and those who are looking after him or her.*

THE LORD'S PRAYER

59   *The minister introduces the Lord's Prayer in these or similar words:*

Now let us offer together the prayer our Lord Jesus
Christ taught us:

All say:
Our Father . . .

CONCLUDING PRAYER

60   *The minister says a concluding prayer. One of the following may be used:*

A
Father,
your Son accepted our sufferings
to teach us the virtue of patience in human illness.
Hear the prayers we offer for our sick brother/sister.
May all who suffer pain, illness, or disease realize
that they have been chosen to be saints and know

that they are joined to Christ in his suffering for the
salvation of the world.

We ask this through Christ our Lord.
R. *Amen.*

B
All-powerful and ever-living God,
the lasting health of all who believe in you,
hear us as we ask your loving help for the sick;
restore their health,
that they may again offer joyful thanks
      in your Church.

Grant this through Christ our Lord.
R. *Amen.*

C
All-powerful and ever-living God,
we find security in your forgiveness.
Give us serenity and peace of mind;
may we rejoice in your gifts of kindness
and use them always for your glory and our good.

We ask this in the name of Jesus the Lord.
R. *Amen.*

BLESSING

61 *The minister may give a blessing. One of the following may be used:*

A

All praise and glory is yours, Lord our God,
for you have called us to serve you in love.
Bless **N.**
so that he/she may bear this illness
in union with your Son's obedient suffering.
Restore him/her to health,
and lead him/her to glory.

We ask this through Christ our Lord.
R. *Amen.*

B

For an elderly person

All praise and glory are yours, Lord our God,
for you have called us to serve you in love.
Bless all who have grown old in your service
and give **N.** strength and courage
to continue to follow Jesus your Son.

We ask this through Christ our Lord.
R. *Amen.*

A minister who is not a priest or deacon invokes God's blessing and makes the sign of the cross on himself or herself, while saying:

May the Lord bless us,
protect us from all evil,
and bring us to everlasting life.
R. Amen.

The minister may then trace the sign of the cross on the sick person's forehead.

Visits to a Sick Child

INTRODUCTION

Let the children come to me; do not keep them back from me.

62   The following readings, prayers, and blessings will help the minister to pray with sick children and their families. They are provided as an example of what can be done and may be adapted as necessary. The minister may wish to invite those present to prepare for the reading from Scripture, perhaps by a brief introduction or through a moment of silence.

63   If the child does not already know the minister, the latter should seek to establish a friendly and easy relationship with the child. Therefore, the greeting which begins the visit should be an informal one.

64   The minister should help sick children to understand that the sick are very special in the eyes of God because they are suffering as Christ suffered and because they can offer their sufferings for the salvation of the world.

65   In praying with the sick child the minister chooses, together with the child and the family if possible, suitable elements of common prayer in the form of a brief liturgy of the word. This may consist of a reading from Scripture, simple one-line prayers taken from Scripture which can be repeated by the child, other familiar prayers such as the Lord's Prayer, the Hail Mary, litanies, or a simple form of the general intercessions. The laying on of hands may be added by the priest, if appropriate, after the child has been blessed.

READING

66   *One of the following readings may be used for a brief liturgy of the word. Other readings may be chosen, for example: Mark 5:21–23, 35–43,* Jesus raises the daughter of Jairus and gives her back to her parents; *Mark 9:14–27,* Jesus cures a boy and gives him back to his father; *Luke 7:11–15,* Jesus raises a young man, the only son of his mother, and gives him back to her; *John 4:46–53,* Jesus gives his second sign by healing an official's son. *In addition, other stories concerning the Lord's healing ministry may be found suitable, especially if told with the simplicity and clarity of one of the children's versions of Scripture.*

A   *Mark 9:33–37*

Jesus proposes the child as the ideal of those who would enter the kingdom.

B   *Mark 10:13–16*
Jesus welcomes the children and lays hands on them.

RESPONSE

67   *After the reading of the word of God, time may be set apart for silent reflection if the child is capable of this form of prayer. The minister should also explain the meaning of the reading to those present, adapting it to their circumstances.*

The minister may then help the child and the family to respond to the word of God. The following short responsory may be used:

Jesus, come to me.

—Jesus, come to me.

Jesus, put your hand on me.

—Jesus, put your hand on me.

Jesus, bless me.

—*Jesus, bless me.*

THE LORD'S PRAYER

68   *The minister introduces the Lord's Prayer in these or similar words:*

Let us pray to the Father using those words which Jesus himself used:

All say:

Our Father . . .

CONCLUDING PRAYER

69   *The minister says a concluding prayer. One of the following may be used.*

A

God of love,
ever caring,
ever strong,
stand by us in our time of need.

Watch over your child **N.** who is sick,
look after him/her in every danger,
and grant him/her your healing and peace.

We ask this in the name of Jesus the Lord.
R. Amen.

B

Father,
in your love
you gave us Jesus
to help us rise triumphant over grief and pain.

Look on your child **N.** who is sick
and see in his/her sufferings those of your Son.

Grant **N.** a share in the strength you granted your Son
that he/she too may be a sign
of your goodness, kindness, and loving care.

We ask this in the name of Jesus the Lord.
R. *Amen.*

BLESSING

70   *The minister makes a sign of the cross on the child's forehead, saying one of the following:*

A

N., when you were baptized,
you were marked with the cross of Jesus.
I (we) make this cross ✚ on your forehead
and ask the Lord to bless you,
and restore you to health.
R. *Amen.*

B

All praise and glory is yours, heavenly God,
for you have called us to serve you in love.
Have mercy on us and listen to our prayer
as we ask you to help **N.**

Bless ✚ your beloved child,
and restore him/her to health
in the name of Jesus the Lord.

R. Amen.

*Each one present may in turn trace the sign of the cross on the child's forehead,
in silence.*

A minister who is not a priest or deacon concludes as described in no. 61.

Communion of the Sick

INTRODUCTION

Whoever eats this bread will live for ever.

71   This chapter contains two rites: one for use when communion can be celebrated in the context of a liturgy of the word; the other, a brief communion rite for use in more restrictive circumstances, such as in hospitals.

72   Priests with pastoral responsibilities should see to it that the sick or aged, even though not seriously ill or in danger of death, are given every opportunity to receive the eucharist frequently, even daily, especially during the Easter season. They may receive communion at any hour. Those who care for the sick may receive communion with them, in accord with the usual norms. To provide frequent communion for the sick, it may be necessary to ensure that the community has a sufficient number of ministers of communion. The communion minister should wear attire appropriate to this ministry.

　　　　The sick person and others may help to plan the celebration, for example, by choosing the prayers and readings. Those making these choices should keep in mind the condition of the sick person. The readings and the homily should help those present to reach a deeper understanding of the mystery of human suffering in relation to the paschal mystery of Christ.

73   The faithful who are ill are deprived of their rightful and accustomed place in the eucharistic community. In bringing communion to them the minister of communion represents Christ and manifests faith and charity on behalf of the whole community toward those who cannot be present at the eucharist. For the sick the reception of communion is not only a privilege

but also a sign of support and concern shown by the Christian community for its members who are ill.

The links between the community's eucharistic celebration, especially on the Lord's Day, and the communion of the sick are intimate and manifold. Besides remembering the sick in the general intercessions at Mass, those present should be reminded occasionally of the significance of communion in the lives of those who are ill: union with Christ in his struggle with evil, his prayer for the world, and his love for the Father, and union with the community from which they are separated.

The obligation to visit and comfort those who cannot take part in the eucharistic assembly may be clearly demonstrated by taking communion to them from the community's eucharistic celebration. This symbol of unity between the community and its sick members has the deepest significance on the Lord's Day, the special day of the eucharistic assembly.

74   When the eucharist is brought to the sick, it should be carried in a pyx or small closed container. Those who are with the sick should be asked to prepare a table covered with a linen cloth upon which the blessed sacrament will be placed. Lighted candles are prepared and, where it is customary, a vessel of holy water. Care should be taken to make the occasion special and joyful.

Sick people who are unable to receive communion under the form of bread may receive it under the form of wine alone. If the wine is consecrated at a Mass not celebrated in the presence of the sick person, the blood of the Lord is kept in a properly covered vessel and is placed in the tabernacle after communion. The precious blood should be carried to the sick in a vessel which is closed in such a way as to eliminate all danger of spilling. If some of the precious blood remains, it should be consumed by the minister, who should also see to it that the vessel is properly purified.

75   If the sick wish to celebrate the sacrament of penance, it is preferable that the priest make himself available for this during a previous visit.

76   If it is necessary to celebrate the sacrament of penance during the rite of communion, it takes the place of the penitential rite.

COMMUNION IN ORDINARY CIRCUMSTANCES

77   If possible, provision should be made to celebrate Mass in the homes of the sick, with their families and friends gathered around them. The Ordinary determines the conditions and requirements for such celebrations.

COMMUNION IN A HOSPITAL OR INSTITUTION

78   There will be situations, particularly in large institutions with many communicants, when the minister should consider alternative means so that the rite of communion of the sick is not diminished to the absolute minimum. In such cases the following alternatives should be considered: (a) where possible, the residents or patients may be gathered in groups in one or more areas; (b) additional ministers of communion may assist.

When it is not possible to celebrate the full rite, the rite for communion in a hospital or institution may be used. If it is convenient, however, the minister may add elements from the rite for ordinary circumstances, for example, a Scripture reading.

79   The rite begins with the recitation of the eucharistic antiphon in the church, the hospital chapel, or the first room visited. Then the minister gives communion to the sick in their individual rooms.

80   The concluding prayer may be said in the church, the hospital chapel, or the last room visited. No blessing is given.

Communion in Ordinary Circumstances

Introductory Rites

Greeting

81   *The minister greets the sick person and the others present. One of the following may be used:*

A

The peace of the Lord be with you always.
R. And also with you.

B

Peace be with you (this house) and with all who live here.
R. And also with you.

C

The grace of our Lord Jesus Christ and the love of God and the fellowship of the Holy Spirit be with you all.
R. And also with you.

D

The grace and peace of God our Father and the Lord
Jesus Christ be with you.
R. *And also with you.*

The minister then places the blessed sacrament on the table and all join in
adoration.

PENITENTIAL RITE

83   *The minister invites the sick person and all present to join in the*
penitential rite, using these or similar words:

A

My brothers and sisters, to prepare ourselves for this
celebration, let us call to mind our sins.

B

My brothers and sisters, let us turn with confidence
to the Lord and ask his forgiveness for all our sins.

After a brief period of silence, the penitential rite continues, using one of the
following:

A

Lord Jesus, you healed the sick:
Lord, have mercy.
R. *Lord, have mercy.*

Lord Jesus, you forgave sinners:
Christ, have mercy.
R. *Christ, have mercy.*

Lord Jesus, you give us yourself to heal us
          and bring us strength:
Lord, have mercy.
R. *Lord, have mercy.*

B
All say:

I confess to almighty God,
and to you, my brothers and sisters,
that I have sinned through my own fault

They strike their breast.
in my thoughts and in my words,
in what I have done,
and in what I have failed to do; ·
and I ask blessed Mary, ever virgin,
all the angels and saints,
and you, my brothers and sisters,
to pray for me to the Lord our God.

The minister concludes the penitential rite with the following:
May almighty God have mercy on us,
forgive us our sins,
and bring us to everlasting life.
R. *Amen.*

LITURGY OF THE WORD
Reading

*84   The word of God is proclaimed by one of those present or by the minister.
An appropriate reading from Part III or one of the following readings may
be used:*

A John 6:51
B John 6:54–58
C John 14:6
D John 15:5
E John 4:16

Response

*85   A brief period of silence may be observed after the reading of the word
of God.*

*The minister may then give a brief explanation of the reading, applying it to the
needs of the sick person and those who are looking after him or her.*

GENERAL INTERCESSIONS

*86   The general intercessions may be said. With a brief introduction the
minister invites all those present to pray. After the intentions the minister says the
concluding prayer. It is desirable that the intentions be announced by someone
other than the minister.*

LITURGY OF HOLY COMMUNION
The Lord's Prayer

87   The minister introduces the Lord's Prayer in these or similar words:

A

Now let us pray as Christ the Lord has taught us:

B

And now let us pray with confidence as Christ our Lord commanded:

All say:

Our Father . . .

Communion

88   *The minister shows the eucharistic bread to those present, saying:*

A

This is the bread of life.
Taste and see that the Lord is good.

B

This is the Lamb of God
who takes away the sins of the world.
Happy are those who are called to his supper.

The sick person and all who are to receive communion say:

Lord, I am not worthy to receive you,
but only say the word and I shall be healed.

The minister goes to the sick person and, showing the blessed sacrament, says:

The body of Christ.

The sick person answers: "Amen," and receives communion.

Then the minister says:

The blood of Christ.

The sick person answers: "Amen," and receives communion.
Others present who wish to receive communion then do so in the usual way.

After the conclusion of the rite, the minister cleanses the vessel as usual.

Silent Prayer

89   *Then a period of silence may be observed.*

Prayer after Communion

90   *The minister says a concluding prayer. One of the following may be used:*

Let us pray.

Pause for silent prayer, if this has not preceded.

A

God our Father,
you have called us to share the one bread
        and one cup
and so become one in Christ.

Help us to live in him
that we may bear fruit,
rejoicing that he has redeemed the world.

We ask this through Christ our Lord.
R. Amen.

B

All-powerful God,
we thank you for the nourishment you give us
through your holy gift.

Pour out your Spirit upon us
and in the strength of this food from heaven
keep us single-minded in your service.

We ask this in the name of Jesus the Lord.
R. Amen.

C

All-powerful and ever-living God,
may the body and blood of Christ your Son
be for our brother/sister **N.**
a lasting remedy for body and soul.

We ask this through Christ our Lord.
R. Amen.

CONCLUDING RITE
Blessing

*91   A minister who is not a priest or deacon invokes God's blessing and
makes the sign of the cross on himself or herself, while saying:*

A

May the Lord bless us,
protect us from all evil,
and bring us to everlasting life.
R. Amen.

B

May the almighty and merciful God bless and
     protect us,
the Father, and the Son, ✚ and the Holy Spirit.
R. Amen.

COMMUNION IN A HOSPITAL OR INSTITUTION

INTRODUCTORY RITE

Antiphon

92   The rite may begin in the church, the hospital chapel, or the first room, where the minister says one of the following antiphons:

A

How holy this feast
in which Christ is our food:
his passion is recalled;
grace fills our hearts;
and we receive a pledge of the glory to come.

B

How gracious you are, Lord:
your gift of bread from heaven
reveals a Father's love and brings us perfect joy.
You fill the hungry with good things
and send the rich away empty.

C

I am the living bread
come down from heaven.
If you eat this bread
you will live for ever.

The bread I will give is my flesh
for the life of the world.

*If it is customary, the minister may be accompanied by a person carrying
a candle.*

LITURGY OF HOLY COMMUNION
Greeting

93   *On entering each room, the minister may use one of the
following greetings:*

A

The peace of the Lord be with you always.
R. *And also with you.*

B

The grace of our Lord Jesus Christ and the love of
God and the fellowship of the Holy Spirit be with
you all.
R. *And also with you.*

*The minister then places the blessed sacrament on the table, and all join
in adoration.*

*If there is time and it seems desirable, the minister may proclaim
a scripture reading from those found in no. 84 or those appearing in Part III.*

The Lord's Prayer

94   *When circumstances permit (for example, when there are not many rooms
to visit), the minister is encouraged to lead the sick in the Lord's Prayer. The
minister introduces the Lord's Prayer in these or similar words:*

A

Jesus taught us to call God our Father, and so we
have the courage to say:

B

Now let us pray as Christ the Lord has taught us:
All say:
Our Father . . .

Communion

95   *The minister shows the eucharistic bread to those present, saying:*

A

This is the Lamb of God
who takes away the sins of the world.
Happy are those who hunger and thirst,
for they shall be satisfied.

B

This it the bread of life,
Taste and see that the Lord is good.

The sick person and all who are to receive communion say:

Lord, I am not worthy to receive you,
but only say the word and I shall be healed.

The minister goes to the sick person and, showing the blessed sacrament, says:

The body of Christ.

The sick person answers: "Amen," and receives communion.

Then the minister says:

The blood of Christ.

The sick person answers: "Amen," and receives communion.

Others present who wish to receive communion then do so in the usual way.

CONCLUDING RITE
Concluding Prayer

96   *The concluding prayer may be said either in the last room visited, in the church, or chapel. One of the following may be used:*

Let us pray.

Pause for silent prayer.

A
God our Father,
you have called us to share the one bread
    and one cup
and so become one in Christ.

Help us to live in him
that we may bear fruit,
rejoicing that he has redeemed the world.

We ask this through Christ our Lord.
R. Amen.

B

All-powerful and ever-living God,
may the body and blood of Christ your Son
be for our brothers and sisters
a lasting remedy for body and soul.
We ask this through Christ our Lord.
R. Amen.

C

All-powerful God,
we thank you for the nourishment you give us
through your holy gift.

Pour out your Spirit upon us
and in the strength of this food from heaven
keep us single-minded in your service.

We ask this in the name of Jesus the Lord.
R. Amen.

The blessing is omitted and the minister cleanses the vessel as usual.

Pastoral Care of the Dying

INTRODUCTION

When we were baptized in Christ Jesus we were baptized into his death . . . so that as Christ was raised from the dead by the Father's glory, we too might live a new life.

161   The rites in Part II of *Pastoral Care of the Sick: Rites of Anointing and Viaticum* are used by the Church to comfort and strengthen a dying Christian in the passage from this life. The ministry to the dying places emphasis on trust in the Lord's promise of eternal life rather than on the struggle against illness which is characteristic of the pastoral care of the sick.

The first three chapters of Part II provide for those situations in which time is not a pressing concern and the rites can be celebrated fully and properly. These are to be clearly distinguished from the rites contained in Chapter Eight, "Rites for Exceptional Circumstances," which provide for the emergency situations sometimes encountered in the ministry to the dying.

162   Priests with pastoral responsibilities are to direct the efforts of the family and friends as well as other ministers of the local Church in the care of the dying. They should ensure that all are familiar with the rites provided here.

The words "priest," "deacon," and "minister" are used advisedly. Only in those rites which must be celebrated by a priest is the word "priest" used in the rubrics (that is, the sacrament of penance, the sacrament of the anointing of the sick, the celebration of viaticum within Mass). Whenever it is clear that, in the absence of a priest, a deacon may preside at a particular rite, the words "priest or deacon," are used in the rubrics. Whenever another minister is permitted to celebrate a rite in the absence of a priest or deacon, the word "minister" is used in the rubrics, even though in many cases the rite will be celebrated by a priest or deacon.

163   The Christian community has a continuing responsibility to pray for and with the person who is dying. Through its sacramental ministry to the dying the community helps Christians to embrace death in mysterious union with the crucified and risen Lord, who awaits them in the fullness of life.

CELEBRATION OF VIATICUM

164   A rite for viaticum within Mass and another for viaticum outside Mass are provided. If possible, viaticum should take place within the full eucharistic celebration, with the family, friends, and other members of the Christian community taking part. The rite for viaticum outside Mass is used when the full eucharistic celebration cannot take place. Again, if it is possible, others should take part.

COMMENDATION OF THE DYING

165   The second chapter of Part II contains a collection of prayers for the spiritual comfort of the Christian who is close to death. These prayers are traditionally called the commendation of the dying to God and are to be used according to the circumstances of each case.

PRAYERS FOR THE DEAD

166   A chapter has also been provided to assist a minister who has been called to attend a person who is already dead. A priest is not to administer the sacrament of anointing. Instead, he should pray for the dead person, using prayers such as those which appear in this chapter. He may find it necessary to explain

to the family of the person who is dead that sacraments are celebrated for the living, not for the dead, and that the dead are effectively helped by the prayers of the living.

RITES FOR EXCEPTIONAL CIRCUMSTANCES

167   Chapter Eight, "Rites for Exceptional Circumstances," contains rites which should be celebrated with a person who has suddenly been placed in proximate or immediate danger of death. They are for emergency circumstances and should be used only when such pressing conditions exist.

CARE OF A DYING CHILD

168   In its ministry to the dying the Church must also respond to the difficult circumstances of a dying child. Although no specific rites appear in Part II for the care of a dying child, these notes are provided to help bring into focus the various aspects of this ministry.

169   When parents learn that their child is dying, they are often bewildered and hurt. In their love for their son or daughter, they may be beset by temptations and doubts and find themselves asking: Why is God taking this child from us? How have we sinned or failed that God would punish us in this way? Why is this innocent child being hurt?

Under these trying circumstances, much of the Church's ministry will be directed to the parents and family. While pain and suffering in an innocent child are difficult for others to bear, the Church helps the parents and family to accept what God has allowed to happen. It should be understood by all beforehand that this process of acceptance will probably extend beyond the death of the child. The concern of the Christian community should continue as long as necessary.

Concern for the child must be equal to that for the family. Those who deal with dying children observe that their faith matures rapidly. Though young children often seem to accept death more easily than adults, they will often experience a surprisingly mature anguish because of the pain which they see in their families.

170   At such a time, it is important for members of the Christian community to come to the support of the child and the family by prayer, visits, and other forms of assistance. Those who have lost children of their own have a ministry of consolation and support to the family. Hospital personnel (doctors, nurses, aides) should also be prepared to exercise a special role with the child as caring adults. Priests and deacons bear particular responsibility for overseeing all these elements of the Church's pastoral ministry. The minister should invite members of the community to use their individual gifts in this work of communal care and concern.

171   By conversation and brief services of readings and prayers, the minister may help the parents and family to see that their child is being called ahead of them to enter the kingdom and joy of the Lord. The period when the child is dying can become a special time of renewal and prayer for the family and close friends. The minister should help them to see that the child's sufferings are united to those of Jesus for the salvation of the whole world.

172   If it is appropriate, the priest should discuss with the parents the possibility of preparing and celebrating with the child the sacraments of initiation (baptism, confirmation, eucharist). The priest may baptize and confirm the child (see *Rite of Confirmation*, no. 7b). To complete the process of initiation, the child should also receive first communion.

According to the circumstances, some of these rites may be celebrated by a deacon or layperson. So that the child and family may receive full benefit from them, these rites are normally celebrated over a period of time. In this case, the minister should use the usual rites, that is, the *Rite of Baptism for Children*, the *Rite of Confirmation*, and if suitable, the *Rite of Penance*. Similarly, if time allows, the usual rites for anointing and viaticum should be celebrated.

173   If sudden illness or an accident has placed an uninitiated child in proximate danger of death, the minister uses "Christian Initiation for the Dying," adapting it for use with a child.

174   For an initiated child or a child lacking only the sacrament of confirmation, who is in proximate danger of death, the "Continuous Rite of Penance, Anointing, and Viaticum" may be used and adapted to the understanding of the child. If death is imminent it should be remembered that viaticum rather than anointing is the sacrament for the dying.

CELEBRATION OF VIATICUM

INTRODUCTION

I am going to prepare a place for you; I shall come back and take you with me.

175   This chapter contains a rite for viaticum within Mass and a rite for viaticum outside Mass. The celebration of the eucharist as viaticum, food for the passage through death to eternal life, is the sacrament proper to the dying Christian. It is the completion and crown of the Christian life on this earth, signifying that the Christian follows the Lord to eternal glory and the banquet of the heavenly kingdom.

The sacrament of the anointing of the sick should be celebrated at the beginning of a serious illness. Viaticum, celebrated when death is close, will then be better understood as the last sacrament of Christian life.

176   Priests and other ministers entrusted with the spiritual care of the sick should do everything they can to ensure that those in proximate danger of death receive the body and blood of Christ as viaticum. At the earliest opportunity, the necessary preparation should be given to the dying person, family, and others who may take part.

177   Whenever it is possible, the dying Christian should be able to receive viaticum within Mass. In this way he or she shares fully, during the final moments of this life, in the eucharistic sacrifice, which proclaims the Lord's own passing through death to life. However, circumstances, such as confinement to a hospital ward or the very emergency which makes death imminent, may frequently make the complete eucharistic celebration impossible.

In this case, the rite for viaticum outside Mass is appropriate. The minister should wear attire appropriate to this ministry.

178   Because the celebration of viaticum ordinarily takes place in the limited circumstances of the home, a hospital, or other institution, the simplifications of the rite for Masses in small gatherings may be appropriate. Depending on the condition of the dying person, every effort should be made to involve him or her, the family, friends, and other members of the local community in the planning and celebration. Appropriate readings, prayers, and songs will help to foster the full participation of all. Because of this concern for participation, the minister should ensure that viaticum is celebrated while the dying person is still able to take part and respond.

179   A distinctive feature of the celebration of viaticum, whether within or outside Mass, is the renewal of the baptismal profession of faith by the dying person. This occurs after the homily and replaces the usual form of the profession of faith. Through the baptismal profession at the end of earthly life, the one who is dying uses the language of his or her initial commitment, which is renewed each Easter and on other occasions in the Christian life. In the context of viaticum, it is a renewal and fulfillment of initiation into the Christian mysteries, baptism leading to the eucharist.

180   The rites for viaticum within and outside Mass may include the sign of peace. The minister and all who are present embrace the dying Christian. In this and in other parts of the celebration the sense of leave-taking need not be concealed or denied, but the joy of Christian hope, which is the comfort and strength of the one near death, should also be evident.

181   As an indication that the reception of the eucharist by the dying Christian is a pledge of resurrection and food for the passage through death, the special words proper to viaticum are added: "May the Lord Jesus Christ protect you and lead you to eternal life." The dying person and all who are present may receive communion under both kinds. The sign of communion is more complete when received in this manner because it expresses more fully and clearly the nature of the eucharist as a meal, one which prepares all who take part in it for the heavenly banquet (see the *General Instruction of the Roman Missal,* no. 240).

The minister should choose the manner of giving communion under both kinds which is suitable in the particular case. If the wine is consecrated at a Mass not celebrated in the presence of the sick person, the blood of the Lord is kept in a properly covered vessel and is placed in the tabernacle after communion. The precious blood should be carried to the sick person in a vessel which is closed in such a way as to eliminate all danger of spilling. If some of the precious blood remains after communion, it should be consumed by the minister, who should also see to it that the vessel is properly purified.

The sick who are unable to receive under the form of bread may receive under the form of wine alone. If the wine is consecrated at a Mass not celebrated in the presence of the sick person, the instructions given above are followed.

182   In addition to these elements of the rites which are to be given greater stress, special texts are provided for the general intercessions or litany and the final solemn blessing.

183   It often happens that a person who has received the eucharist as viaticum lingers in a grave condition or at the point of death for a period of days or longer. In these circumstances he or she should be given the opportunity to receive the eucharist

as viaticum on successive days, frequently if not daily. This may take place during or outside Mass as particular conditions permit. The rite may be simplified according to the condition of the one who is dying.

VIATICUM WITHIN MASS

184   When viaticum is received within Mass, the ritual Mass for Viaticum or the Mass of the Holy Eucharist may be celebrated. The priest wears white vestments. The readings may be taken from *The Lectionary for Mass* (second edition, nos. 796–800), unless the dying person and those involved with the priest in planning the liturgy choose other readings from Scripture.

A ritual Mass is not permitted during the Easter triduum, on the solemnities of Christmas, Epiphany, Ascension, Pentecost, Corpus Christi, or on a solemnity which is a holy day of obligation. On these occasions, the texts and readings are taken from the Mass of the day. Although the Mass for Viaticum or the Mass of the Holy Eucharist are also excluded on the Sundays of Advent, Lent, and the Easter season, on solemnities, Ash Wednesday, and the weekdays of Holy Week, one of the readings may be taken from the biblical texts indicated above. The special form of the final blessing may be used and, at the discretion of the priest, the apostolic pardon may be added.

185   If the dying person wishes to celebrate the sacrament of penance, it is preferable that the priest make himself available for this during a previous visit. If this is not possible, the sacrament of penance may be celebrated before Mass begins (see Appendix, p. 372).

VIATICUM OUTSIDE MASS

186   Although viaticum celebrated in the context of the full eucharistic celebration is always preferable, when it is not

possible the rite for viaticum outside Mass is appropriate. This rite includes some of the elements of the Mass, especially a brief liturgy of the word. Depending on the circumstances and the condition of the dying person, this rite should also be a communal celebration. Every effort should be made to involve the dying person, family, friends, and members of the local community in the planning and celebration. The manner of celebration and the elements of the rite which are used should be accommodated to those present and the nearness of death.

187   If the dying person wishes to celebrate the sacrament of penance and this cannot take place during a previous visit, it should be celebrated before the rite of viaticum begins, especially if others are present. Alternatively, it may be celebrated during the rite of viaticum, replacing the penitential rite. At the discretion of the priest, the apostolic pardon may be added after the penitential rite or after the sacrament of penance.

188   An abbreviated liturgy of the word, ordinarily consisting of a single biblical reading, gives the minister an opportunity to explain the word of God in relation to viaticum. The sacrament should be described as the sacred food which strengthens the Christian for the passage through death to life in sure hope of the resurrection.

VIATICUM OUTSIDE MASS

INTRODUCTORY RITES

Greeting

197   The minister greets the sick person and the others present. The following may be used:

A

The peace of the Lord be with you always.
R. And also with you.

B

Peace be with you (this house) and with all who
live here.
R. And also with you.

C

The grace of our Lord Jesus Christ and the love of
God and the fellowship of the Holy Spirit be with
you all.
R. And also with you.

D

The grace and peace of God our Father and the Lord
Jesus Christ be with you.
R. And also with you.

The minister then places the blessed sacrament on the table, and all join in adoration.

Instruction

199   Afterward the minister addresses those present, using the following instruction or one better suited to the sick person's condition:

My brothers and sisters, before our Lord Jesus Christ passed from this world to return to the Father, he left us the sacrament of his body and blood. When the hour comes for us to pass from this life and join him, he strengthens us with this food for our journey and comforts us by this pledge of our resurrection.

Penitential Rite

200   The minister invites the sick person and all present to join in the penitential rite, using these or similar words:

A

My brothers and sisters, to prepare ourselves for this celebration, let us call to mind our sins.

B

My brothers and sisters, let us turn with confidence to the Lord and ask his forgiveness for all our sins.

After a brief period of silence, the penitential rite continues using one of the following prayers.

A   *All say:*

I confess to almighty God,
and to you, my brothers and sisters,
that I have sinned through my own fault

They strike their breast.

in my thoughts and in my words,
in what I have done,
and in what I have failed to do;
and I ask blessed Mary, every virgin,
all the angels and saints,
and you, my brothers and sisters,
to pray for me to the Lord our God.

B

By your paschal mystery
        you have won for us salvation:
Lord, have mercy.
R. *Lord, have mercy.*

You renew among us now
        the wonders of your passion:
Christ, have mercy.
R. *Christ, have mercy.*

When we receive your body,
you share with us your paschal sacrifice:
Lord, have mercy.
R. *Lord, have mercy.*

The minister concludes the penitential rite with the following:

May almighty God have mercy us,
forgive us our sins,
and bring us to everlasting life.
R. Amen.

LITURGY OF THE WORD

Reading

202   *The word of God is proclaimed by one of those present or by the minister.*
An appropriate reading from Part III or one of the following may be used:

A John 6:54–55
B John 14:23
C John 15:4
D I Corinthians 11:26

Homily

203   *Depending on circumstances, the minister may then give a brief*
explanation of the reading.

Baptismal Profession of Faith

204   *It is desirable that the sick person renew his or her baptismal profession*
of faith before receiving viaticum. The minister gives a brief introduction and then
asks the following questions:

N., do you believe in God, the Father almighty,
creator of heaven and earth?
R. I do.

Do you believe in Jesus Christ, his only Son, our Lord,
who was born of the Virgin Mary,

was crucified, died, and was buried,
rose from the dead,
and is now seated at the right hand of the Father?
R. I do.

Do you believe in the Holy Spirit,
the holy catholic Church, the communion of saints,
the forgiveness of sins, the resurrection of the body,
and life everlasting?
R. I do.

Litany

205   *The minister may adapt or shorten the litany according to the condition of the sick person. The litany may be omitted if the sick person has made the profession of faith and appears to be tiring.*

My brothers and sisters, with one heart let us call on our Savior Jesus Christ.

You loved us to the very end and gave yourself over to death in order to give us life. For our brother/sister, Lord, we pray:
R. Lord, hear our prayer.

You said to us: "All who eat my flesh and drink my blood will live for ever." For our brother/sister, Lord, we pray:
R. Lord, hear our prayer.

You invite us to join in the banquet where pain and sorrow, sadness and separation will be no more. For our brother/sister, Lord, we pray:
R. Lord, hear our prayer.

LITURGY OF VIATICUM

The Lord's Prayer

206   The minister introduces the Lord's Prayer in these words:

A

Now let us offer together the prayer our Lord Jesus
Christ taught us:

B

And now let us pray with confidence as Christ our
Lord commanded:

All say:

Our Father . . .

Communion as Viaticum

*207   The sick person and all present may receive communion under both kinds.
When the minister gives communion to the sick person, the form for viaticum
is used.*

The minister shows the eucharistic bread to those present, saying:

A

Jesus Christ is the food for our journey;
he calls us to the heavenly table.

B

This is the bread of life.
Taste and see that the Lord is good.

The sick person and all who are to receive communion say:

Lord, I am not worthy to receive you,
but only say the word and I shall be healed.

The minister goes to the sick person and, showing the blessed sacrament, says:

The body of Christ.

The sick person answers: "Amen."

Then the minister says:

The blood of Christ.

The sick person answers: "Amen."

Immediately, or after giving communion to the sick person, the minister adds:

May the Lord Jesus Christ protect you
and lead you to eternal life.
R. Amen.

Others present who wish to receive communion then do so in the usual way.

After the conclusion of the rite, the minister cleanses the vessel as usual.

Silent Prayer

208   *Then a period of silence may be observed.*

Prayer after Communion

209   *The minister says the concluding prayer.*

Let us pray.

Pause for silent prayer, if this has not preceded.

A.

God of peace,
you offer eternal healing to those who believe in you;
you have refreshed your servant **N.**
with food and drink from heaven:
lead him/her safely into the kingdom of light.

We ask this through Christ our Lord.
R. Amen.

B

All-powerful and ever-living God,
may the body and blood of Christ your Son
be for our brother/sister N.
a lasting remedy for body and soul.

We ask this through Christ our Lord.
R. Amen.

C

Father,
your son, Jesus Christ, is our way, our truth,
        and our life.
Look with compassion on your servant N.
who has trusted in your promises.
You have refreshed him/her with the body and blood
        of your Son:
may he/she enter your kingdom in peace.

We ask this through Christ our Lord.

R. Amen.

CONCLUDING RITES

Blessing

210   A minister who is not a priest or deacon invokes God's blessing and makes the sign of the cross on himself or herself, while saying:

May the Lord bless us,
protect us from all evil,
and bring us to everlasting life.

R. Amen.

Sign of Peace

211   The minister and the others present may then give the sick person the sign of peace.

Commendation of the Dying

INTRODUCTION

Into your hands, Lord, I commend my spirit.

212   In viaticum the dying person is united with Christ in his passage out of this world to the Father. Through the prayers for the commendation of the dying contained in this chapter, the Church helps to sustain this union until it is brought to fulfillment after death.

213   Christians have the responsibility of expressing their union in Christ by joining the dying person in prayer for God's mercy and for confidence in Christ. In particular, the presence of a priest or deacon shows more clearly that the Christian dies in the communion of the Church. He should assist the dying person and those present in the recitation of the prayers of commendation and, following death, he should lead those present in the prayer after death. If the priest or deacon is unable to be present because of other serious pastoral obligations, other members of the community should be prepared to assist with these prayers and should have the texts readily available to them.

214   The minister may choose texts from among the prayers, litanies, aspirations, psalms, and readings provided in this chapter, or others may be added. In the selection of these texts the minister should keep in mind the condition and piety of both the dying person and the members of the family who are present. The prayers are best said in a slow, quiet voice, alternating with periods of silence. If possible, the minister says one or more of

the brief prayer formulas with the dying person. These may be softly repeated two or three times.

215   These texts are intended to help the dying person, if still conscious, to face the natural human anxiety about death by imitating Christ in his patient suffering and dying. The Christian will be helped to surmount his or her fear in the hope of heavenly life and resurrection through the power of Christ, who destroyed the power of death by his own dying.

Even if the dying person is not conscious, those who are present will draw consolation from these prayers and come to a better understanding of the paschal character of Christian death. This may be visibly expressed by making the sign of the cross on the forehead of the dying person, who was first signed with the cross at baptism.

216   Immediately after death has occurred, all may kneel while one of those present leads the prayers given on nos. 221–222.

SHORT TEXTS

217   One or more of the following short texts may be recited with the dying person. If necessary, they may be softly repeated two or three times.

Romans 8:35
Who can separate us from the love of Christ?

Romans 14:8
Whether we live or die, we are the Lord's.

2 Corinthians 5:1
We have an everlasting home in heaven.

1 Thessalonians 4:17
We shall be with the Lord for ever.

1 John 3:2
We shall see God as he really is.

1 John 3:14
We have passed from death to life
because we love each other.

Psalm 25:1
To you, Lord, I lift up my soul.

Psalm 27:1
The Lord is my light and my salvation.

Psalm 27:13
I believe that I shall see the goodness of the Lord
in the land of the living.

Psalm 42:3
My soul thirsts for the living God.

Psalm 23:4
Though I walk in the shadow of death,
I will fear no evil,
for you are with me.

Matthew 25:34
Come, blessed of my Father,
says the Lord Jesus,
and take possession of the kingdom
prepared for you.

Luke 23:43
The Lord Jesus says,
today you will be with me in paradise.

John 14:2
In my Father's home
there are many dwelling places,
says the Lord Jesus.

John 14:2-3
The Lord Jesus says,
I go to prepare a place for you,
and I will come again to take you to myself.

John 17:24
I desire that where I am,
they also may be with me,
says the Lord Jesus.

John 6:40
Everyone who believes in the Son
has eternal life.

Psalm 31:5a
Into your hands, Lord,
I commend my spirit.

Acts 7:59
Lord Jesus, receive my spirit.

Holy Mary, pray for me.

Saint Joseph, pray for me.

Jesus, Mary, and Joseph,
assist me in my last agony.

READING

218   *The word of God is proclaimed by one of those present or by the minister.*
Selections from Part III or from the following readings may be used:

A *Job 19:23–27a*
Job's act of faith is a model for our own; God is the God of the living.

B *Psalm 23*
C *Psalm 25*
D *Psalm 91*
E *Psalm 121*
F *1 John 4:16*

G *Revelation 21:1–5a, 6–7*
God our Father is the God of newness of life; it is his desire that we
should come to share his life with him.

H *Matthew 25:1–13*
Jesus bid us be prepared for our ultimate destiny, which is eternal life.

I Luke 22:39-46
Jesus is alive to our pain and sorrow, because faithfulness to his Father's will cost him life itself.

J Luke 24:1-8
Jesus' death is witnessed by his friends.

K Luke 24:1-8
Jesus is alive; he gives us eternal life with the Father.

L John 6:37-40
Jesus will raise his own from death and give them eternal life.

M John 14:1-6, 23, 27
The love of Jesus can raise us up from the sorrow of death to the joy of eternal life.

Litany of the Saints

219   *When the condition of the dying person calls for the use of brief forms of prayer, those who are present are encouraged to pray the litany of the saints— or at least some of its invocations—for him or her. Special mention may be made of the patron saints of the dying person, of the family, and of the parish. The litany may be said or sung in the usual way. Other customary prayers may also be used.*

Lord, have mercy . . . . .Lord, have mercy
Christ, have mercy . . . . Christ, have mercy
Lord, have mercy . . . . Lord, have mercy

Holy Mary, Mother of God . . . . pray for him/her
Holy angels of God . . . . pray for him/her
Abraham, our father in faith . . . . . . pray for him/her
David, leader of God's people . . . . . pray for him/her
All holy patriarchs and prophets . . . pray for him/her

Saint John the Baptist . . . . pray for him/her
Saint Joseph . . . . pray for him/her
Saint Peter and Saint Paul . . . . pray for him/her

Saint Andrew . . . . pray for him/her
Saint John. . . . . pray for him/her
Saint Mary Magdalene . . . . pray for him/her
Saint Stephen . . . . pray for him/her
Saint Ignatius . . . . pray for him/her
Saint Lawrence . . . . pray for him/her
Saint Perpetua and Saint Felicity. . . pray for him/her
Saint Agnes . . . . pray for him/her
Saint Gregory . . . . pray for him/her
Saint Augustine . . . . pray for him/her
Saint Athanasius. . . . . pray for him/her
Saint Basil . . . . pray for him/her
Saint Martin . . . . pray for him/her
Saint Benedict. . . . . pray for him/her
Saint Francis and Saint Dominic . . . pray for him/her
Saint Francis Xavier . . . . pray for him/her
Saint John Vianney . . . . pray for him/her
Saint Catherine. . . . . pray for him/her
Saint Teresa . . . . pray for him/her

Other saints may be included here.

All holy men and women . . . . pray for him/her

Lord, be merciful. . . . . Lord, save your people
From all evil . . . . Lord, save your people
From every sin . . . . Lord, save your people
From Satan's power . . . . Lord, save your people
At the moment of death. . . . . Lord, save your people
From everlasting death . . . . . Lord, save your people
On the day of judgment. . . . . Lord, save your people
By your coming as man . . . . Lord, save your people

By your suffering and cross. . Lord, save your people
By your death
        and rising to new life . . Lord, save your people
By your return in glory
        to the Father . . . . Lord, save your people
By your gift
        of the Holy Spirit . . . . . Lord, save your people
By your coming again
        in glory . . . . Lord, save your people

Be merciful to us sinners. . . . . Lord, hear our prayer
Bring N. to eternal life,
        first promised to
        him/her in baptism. . . . Lord, hear our prayer
Raise N. on the last day,
        for he/she has eaten
        the bread of life . . . . . . Lord, hear our prayer
Let N. share in your glory,
        for he/she has shared in
        your suffering and death Lord, hear our prayer
Jesus, Son of the living God . . Lord, hear our prayer
Christ, hear us . . . . Christ, hear us
Lord Jesus, hear our prayer. . . Lord, hear our prayer

B

*A brief form of the litany may be prayed. Other saints may be added, including
the patron saints of the dying person, of the family, and of the parish; saints to
whom the dying person may have a special devotion may also be included.*

Holy Mary, Mother of God . . . . pray for him/her
Holy angels of God . . . . pray for him/her
Saint John the Baptist . . . . pray for him/her
Saint Joseph . . . . pray for him/her
Saint Peter and Saint Paul . . . . pray for him/her

Other saints may be included here.

All holy men and women . . . . pray for him/her

Prayer of Commendation

220   *When the moment of death seems near, some of the following prayers
may be said:*

A

Go forth, Christian soul, from this world
in the name of God the almighty Father,
who created you,
in the name of Jesus Christ, Son of the living God,
who suffered for you,
in the name of the Holy Spirit,
who was poured out upon you,
go forth, faithful Christian.

May you live in peace this day,
may your home be with God in Zion,
with Mary, the virgin Mother of God,
with Joseph, and all the angels and saints.

B

I commend you, my dear brother/sister,
to almighty God,
and entrust you to your Creator.
May you return to him
who formed you from the dust of the earth.
May holy Mary, the angels, and all the saints
come to meet you as you go forth from this life.
May Christ who was crucified for you
bring you freedom and peace.
May Christ who died for you
admit you into his garden of paradise.
May Christ, the true Shepherd,
acknowledge you as one of his flock.
May he forgive all your sins,
and set you among those he has chosen.
May you see your Redeemer face to face,
and enjoy the vision of God for ever.
R. Amen.

C

Welcome your servant, Lord, into the place of
salvation which because of your mercy he/she
rightly hoped for.
R. Amen, or R. Lord, save your people.

Deliver your servant, Lord, from every distress.
R. Amen, or R. Lord, save your people.

Deliver your servant, Lord, as you delivered Noah from the flood.
R. Amen, or R. Lord, save your people.

Deliver your servant, Lord, as you delivered Abraham from Ur of the Chaldees.
R. Amen, or R. Lord, save your people.

Deliver your servant, Lord, as you delivered Moses from the hand of the Pharaoh.
R. Amen, or R. Lord, save your people.

Deliver your servant, Lord, as you delivered Daniel from the den of lions.
R. Amen, or R. Lord, save your people.

Deliver your servant, Lord, as you delivered the three young men from the fiery furnace.
R. Amen, or R. Lord, save your people.

Deliver your servant, Lord, as you delivered Susanna from her false accusers.
R. Amen, or R. Lord, save your people.

Deliver your servant, Lord, as you delivered David from the attacks of Saul and Goliath.
R. Amen, or R. Lord, save your people.

Deliver your servant, Lord, as you delivered Peter and Paul from prison.
R. Amen, or R. Lord, save your people.

Deliver your servant, Lord, through Jesus our Savior,
who suffered death for us and gave us eternal life.
R. *Amen,* or R. *Lord, save your people.*

D

Lord Jesus Christ, Savior of the world,
we pray for your servant N.,
and commend him/her to your mercy.
For his/sake you came down from heaven;
receive him/her now into the joy of your kingdom.

For though he/she has sinned,
he she/has not denied the Father, the Son,
    and the Holy Spirit,
but has believed in God
and has worshipped his/her Creator.
R. *Amen.*

E   *The following antiphon may be said or sung:*

Hail, holy Queen, Mother of mercy,
hail, our life, our sweetness, and our hope.
To you we cry, the children of Eve;
to you we send up our sighs,
mourning and weeping in this land of exile.
Turn, then, most gracious advocate,
your eyes of mercy toward us;
lead us home at last

and show us the blessed fruit of your womb, Jesus:
O clement, O loving, O sweet Virgin Mary.

Prayer after Death

221   *When death has occurred, one or more of the following prayers may be said:*

A

Saints of God, come to his/her aid!
Come to meet him/her, angels of the Lord!
R. *Receive his/her soul and present him/her to God the Most High.*

May Christ, who called you, take you to himself; may angels lead you to Abraham's side.
R. *Receive his/her soul and present him/her to God the Most High.*

Give him/her eternal rest, O Lord,
and may your light shine on him/her for ever.
R. *Receive his/her soul and present him/her to God the Most High.*

The following prayer is added:
Let us pray.

All-powerful and merciful God,
we commend to you N., your servant.

In your mercy and love,
blot out the sins he/she has committed
　　　through human weakness.
In this world he/she has died:
let him/her live with you for ever.

We ask this through Christ our Lord.
R. Amen.

*For the solace of those present the minister may conclude these prayers with
a simple blessing or with a symbolic gesture, for example, signing the forehead
with the sign of the cross.*

B　Psalm 130

R. My soul hopes in the Lord.

Out of the depths I cry to you, O Lord;
　　　Lord, hear my voice!
Let your ears be attentive
　　　to my voice in supplication.
R. My soul hopes in the Lord.

I trust in the Lord,
　　　my soul trusts in his word.
My soul waits for the Lord
　　　more than sentinels wait for the dawn.
R. My soul hopes in the Lord.

For with the Lord is kindness,
　　　and with him is plenteous redemption.

And he will redeem Israel
> from all their iniquities.

R. My soul hopes in the Lord.

The following prayer is added:
Let us pray.
God of love, welcome into your presence
your son/daughter *N.*, whom you have
> called from this life.

Release him/her from all his/her sins,
bless him/her with eternal light and peace,
raise him/her up to live for ever with all your saints
in the glory of the resurrection.

We ask this through Christ our Lord.

R. Amen.

C PSALM 23

R. Lord, remember me in your kingdom.

The LORD is my shepherd; I shall not want.
> In verdant pastures he gives me repose;

Beside restful waters he leads me;
> he refreshes my soul.

R. Lord, remember me in your kingdom.

He guides me in right paths
> for his name's sake.

Even though I walk in the dark valley
    I fear no evil; for you are at my side
With your rod and your staff
    that give me courage.
R. Lord, remember me in your kingdom.

You spread the table before me
    in the sight of my foes;
You anoint my head with oil;
    my cup overflows.
R. Lord, remember me in your kingdom.

Only goodness and kindness follow me
    all the days of my life;
And I shall dwell in the house of the LORD
    for years to come.
R. Lord, remember me in your kingdom.

The following prayer is added:
Let us pray.
God of mercy,
hear our prayers and be merciful
to your son/daughter *N.*,
    whom you have called from this life.
Welcome him/her into the company of your saints,
in the kingdom of light and peace.

We ask this through Christ our Lord.
R. Amen.

D

Almighty and eternal God,
hear our prayers for your son/daughter N.,
whom you have called from this life to yourself.

Grant him/her light, happiness, and peace.
Let him/her pass in safety through the gates
of death,
and live for ever with all your saints
in the light you promised to Abraham
and to all his descendants in faith.

Guard him/her from all harm
and on that great day of resurrection and reward
raise him/her up with all your saints.
Pardon his/her sins
and give him/her eternal life in your kingdom.

We ask this through Christ our Lord.
R. Amen.

E

Loving and merciful God,
we entrust our brother/sister to your mercy.
You loved him/her greatly in this life:
now that he/she is freed from all its cares,
give him/her happiness and peace for ever.

The old order has passed away:
welcome him/her now into paradise

where there will be no more sorrow,
no more weeping or pain,
but only peace and joy
with Jesus, your Son,
and the Holy Spirit
for ever and ever.
R. Amen.

F

God of our destiny,
into your hands we commend our brother/sister.
We are confident that with all who have died in Christ
he/she will be raised to life on the last day
and live with Christ for ever.

[We thank you for all the blessings
you gave him/her in this life
to show your fatherly care for all of us
and the fellowship which is ours with the saints
in Jesus Christ.]

Lord, hear our prayer:
welcome our brother/sister to paradise
and help us to comfort each other
with the assurance of our faith
until we all meet in Christ
to be with you and with our brother/sister for ever.

We ask this through Christ our Lord.
R. Amen.

Prayer for the Family and Friends

222 *The following prayer may be said:*

Let us pray.

A   *For the family and friends*

A God of all consolation,
in your unending love and mercy for us
you turn the darkness of death
into the dawn of new life.
Show compassion to your people in their sorrow.

[Be our refuge and our strength
to lift us from the darkness of this grief
to the peace and light of your presence.]

Your Son, our Lord Jesus Christ,
by dying for us, conquered death
and by rising again, restored life.

May we then go forward eagerly to meet him,
and after our life on earth
be reunited with our brothers and sisters
where every tear will be wiped away.
We ask this through Christ our Lord.
R. *Amen.*

B   *For the deceased person and for family and friends*

Lord Jesus, our Redeemer,
you willingly gave yourself up to death
so that all people might be saved

and pass from death into new life.
Listen to our prayers,
look with love on your people
who mourn and pray for their brother/sister **N.**

Lord Jesus, holy and compassionate:
forgive **N.** his/her sins.
By dying you opened the gates of life
for those who believe in you:
do not let our brother/sister be parted from you,
but by your glorious power
give him/her light, joy, and peace in heaven
where you live for ever and ever.
R. *Amen.*

For the solace of those present the minister may conclude these prayers with
a simple blessing or with a symbolic gesture, for example, signing the forehead
with the sign of the cross.

Prayers for the Dead

INTRODUCTION

I want those you have given me to be with me where I am.

223   This chapter contains prayers for use by a minister who has been called to attend a person who is already dead. A priest is not to administer the sacraments of penance or anointing. Instead, he should pray for the dead person using these or similar prayers.

224   It may be necessary to explain to the family of the person who is dead that sacraments are celebrated for the living, not for the dead, and that the dead are effectively helped by the prayers of the living.

225   To comfort those present the minister may conclude these prayers with a simple blessing or with a symbolic gesture, for example, making the sign of the cross on the forehead. A priest or deacon may sprinkle the body with holy water.

Greeting

226   *The minister greets those who are present, offering them sympathy and the consolation of faith, using the following or similar words:*

A

In this moment of sorrow
the Lord is in our midst
and comforts us with his word:
Blessed are the sorrowful; they shall be consoled.

B

Praised be God, the Father of our Lord Jesus Christ,
the Father of mercies,
and the God of all consolation!
He comforts us in all our afflictions
and thus enables us to comfort those who are
      in trouble,
with the same consolation
we have received from him.

Prayer

227   *The minister then says one of the following prayers, commending the*
person who has just died to God's mercy and goodness:

Let us pray.

A

Almighty and eternal God,
hear our prayers for your son/daughter N.,
whom you have called from this life to yourself.

Grant him/her light, happiness, and peace.
Let him/her pass in safety through the gates
      of death,
and live for ever with all your saints
in the light you promised to Abraham
and to all his descendants in faith.

Guard him/her from all harm
and on that great day of resurrection and reward
raise him/her up with all your saints.

Pardon his/her sins
and give him/her eternal life in your kingdom.

We ask this through Christ our Lord.
R. Amen.

B
Loving and merciful God,
we entrust our brother/sister to your mercy.
You loved him/her greatly in this life:
now that he/she is freed from all its cares,
give him/her happiness and peace for ever.

The old order has passed away:
welcome him/her now into paradise
where there will be no more sorrow,
no more weeping or pain,
but only peace and joy
with Jesus, your Son,
and the Holy Spirit
for ever and ever.
R. Amen.

Reading

228   *The word of God is proclaimed by one of those present or by the minister.*
One of the following readings may be used:

A Luke 23:44–46
B John 11:3–7, 20–27, 33–36, 41–44

Litany

229 *Then one of those present may lead the others in praying a brief form of the litany of the saints. (The full form of the litany of the saints may be found in no. 219.) Other saints may be added, including the patron saints of the dead person, of the family, and of the parish; saints to whom the deceased person may have had a special devotion may also be included.*

Saints of God, come to his/her aid!
Come to meet him/her, angels of the Lord!

Holy Mary, Mother of God	*pray for him/her*
Saint Joseph	*pray for him/her*
Saint Peter and Saint Paul	*pray for him/her*

The following prayer is added:

God of mercy,
hear our prayers and be merciful
to your son/daughter N., whom you have called
    from this life.
Welcome him/her into the company of your saints,
in the kingdom of light and peace.

We ask this through Christ our Lord.
R. Amen.

The Lord's Prayer

230 *The minister introduces the Lord's Prayer in these or similar words:*

A
With God there is mercy and fullness of redemption;
let us pray as Jesus taught us to pray:

B

Let us pray for the coming of the kingdom as Jesus taught us:

All say:

Our Father . . .

Prayer of Commendation

231   *The minister then concludes with the following prayer:*

Lord Jesus, our Redeemer,
you willingly gave yourself up to death
so that all people might be saved
and pass from death into a new life.
Listen to our prayers,
look with love on your people
who mourn and pray for their brother/sister **N.**

Lord Jesus, holy and compassionate:
forgive **N.** his/her sins.
By dying you opened the gates of life
for those who believe in you:
do not let our brother/sister be parted from you,
but by your glorious power
give him/her light, joy, and peace in heaven
where you live for ever and ever.
R. *Amen.*

*For the solace of those present the minister may conclude these prayers with
a simple blessing or with a symbolic gesture, for example, signing the forehead
with the sign of the cross.*

THE GOSPEL FOR SUNDAYS AND HOLY DAYS OF OBLIGATION

ADVENT

November 29, 2009

FIRST SUNDAY OF ADVENT

A reading from the holy Gospel according to Luke
21:25–28, 34–36

Jesus said to his disciples:
"There will be signs in the sun, the moon,
    and the stars,
  and on earth nations will be in dismay,
    perplexed by the roaring of the sea and the waves.
People will die of fright
  in anticipation of what is coming upon the world,
  for the powers of the heavens will be shaken.
And then they will see the Son of Man
  coming in a cloud with power and great glory.
But when these signs begin to happen,
  stand erect and raise your heads
  because your redemption is at hand.

"Beware that your hearts do not become drowsy
  from carousing and drunkenness
  and the anxieties of daily life,
  and that day catch you by surprise like a trap.

For that day will assault everyone
who lives on the face of the earth.
Be vigilant at all times
and pray that you have the strength
to escape the tribulations that are imminent
and to stand before the Son of Man."

The Gospel of the Lord.

EXPLANATION OF THE READING

The word *Advent* means "coming." The Church gives us this season to reflect on two different kinds of "coming": the coming of Jesus in our human flesh more than two thousand years ago, and the coming of Jesus at the end of time. Today's Gospel gives a terrifying picture of that second coming. Earth and heaven shaken, oceans in upheaval, people in terror and distress: how can we possibly prepare for that day? The answer Jesus gives is quite simple. We must not get totally absorbed in the ordinary, the "anxieties of daily life." The Christian must live with one eye fixed on eternity. The Advent season is a time to work on this new kind of vision.

December 6, 2008

SECOND SUNDAY OF ADVENT

A reading from the holy Gospel according to Luke   *3:1–6*

In the fifteenth year of the reign of Tiberius Caesar,
when Pontius Pilate was governor of Judea,
and Herod was tetrarch of Galilee,
and his brother Philip tetrarch of the region of
Ituraea and Trachonitis,
and Lysanias was tetrarch of Abilene,

during the high priesthood of Annas and Caiaphas,
the word of God came to John the son of Zechariah
in the desert.
John went throughout the whole region of the Jordan,
proclaiming a baptism of repentance for
the forgiveness of sins,
as it is written in the book of the words of
the prophet Isaiah:
A voice of one crying out in the desert:
"Prepare the way of the Lord,
make straight his paths.
Every valley shall be filled
and every mountain and hill shall be made low.
The winding roads shall be made straight,
and the rough ways made smooth,
and all flesh shall see the salvation of God."

The Gospel of the Lord.

EXPLANATION OF THE READING

John the Baptist comes to point the way to the Lord—not a roundabout
or meandering way, but a direct way, a way that levels mountains and fills
valleys, a way that takes us straight to God. How do we follow this road?
It is simple, but not easy. It starts with repentance, a change of heart, and
it leads to forgiveness in the waters of Baptism. That pattern of conversion
is not something we can do once and be done with it. It must become the
insistent pattern of our lives. No matter how many times we lose ourselves
among the "winding roads" and the "rough ways," we must have the
courage—and the humility—to turn again to the path that will lead us
straight to God.

December 8, 2009

Solemnity of the Immaculate Conception of the Blessed Virgin Mary

A reading from the holy Gospel according to Luke

1:26–38

The angel Gabriel was sent from God
   to a town of Galilee called Nazareth,
   to a virgin betrothed to a man named Joseph,
   of the house of David,
   and the virgin's name was Mary.
And coming to her, he said,
   "Hail, full of grace! The Lord is with you."
But she was greatly troubled at what was said
   and pondered what sort of greeting this might be.
Then the angel said to her,
   "Do not be afraid, Mary,
   for you have found favor with God.
Behold, you will conceive in your womb and bear
      a son,
   and you shall name him Jesus.
He will be great and will be called Son of
      the Most High,
   and the Lord God will give him the throne of David
      his father,
   and he will rule over the house of Jacob forever,
   and of his Kingdom there will be no end."

But Mary said to the angel,
"How can this be,
since I have no relations with a man?"

And the angel said to her in reply,
"The Holy Spirit will come upon you,
and the power of the Most High will
overshadow you.
Therefore the child to be born
will be called holy, the Son of God.
And behold, Elizabeth, your relative,
has also conceived a son in her old age,
and this is the sixth month for her who was
called barren;
for nothing will be impossible for God."
Mary said, "Behold, I am the handmaid of the Lord.
May it be done to me according to your word."
Then the angel departed from her.

The Gospel of the Lord.

EXPLANATION OF THE READING

Gabriel's greeting is first met with fear, pondering, and wonderment. Yet, in the promise of the Spirit, Mary surrenders herself to all that God asks. This woman, graced by God, responds in grace to God's intimate invitation. We stand with Gabriel and declare Mary to be full of grace, trusting that our proclamation itself is enabled by grace.

December 13, 2009

THIRD SUNDAY OF ADVENT

A reading from the holy Gospel according to Luke

3:10–18

The crowds asked John the Baptist,
  "What should we do?"
He said to them in reply,
  "Whoever has two cloaks
  should share with the person who has none.
And whoever has food should do likewise."
Even tax collectors came to be baptized and they
    said to him,
  "Teacher, what should we do?"
He answered them,
  "Stop collecting more than what is prescribed."
Soldiers also asked him,
  "And what is it that we should do?"
He told them,
  "Do not practice extortion,
  do not falsely accuse anyone,
  and be satisfied with your wages."

Now the people were filled with expectation,
  and all were asking in their hearts
  whether John might be the Christ.
John answered them all, saying,
  "I am baptizing you with water,
  but one mightier than I is coming.

I am not worthy to loosen the thongs of his sandals.
He will baptize you with the Holy Spirit and fire.
His winnowing fan is in his hand to clear his
     threshing floor
   and to gather the wheat into his barn,
   but the chaff he will burn with unquenchable fire."
Exhorting them in many other ways,
   he preached good news to the people.

The Gospel of the Lord.

EXPLANATION OF THE READING

John's ministry penetrated people's hearts to the degree that they wondered about the ways their lives needed to change. As John concretely responds to tax collectors and soldiers, he announces the coming of the one who will baptize in the power of the Holy Spirit. God's word challenges us to new patterns of justice and mercy, while God's Spirit enables us to live this new way of being.

December 20, 2009

FOURTH SUNDAY OF ADVENT

A reading from the holy Gospel according to Luke

1:39–45

Mary set out
   and traveled to the hill country in haste
   to a town of Judah,
   where she entered the house of Zechariah
   and greeted Elizabeth.

When Elizabeth heard Mary's greeting,
the infant leaped in her womb,
and Elizabeth, filled with the Holy Spirit,
cried out in a loud voice and said,
"Blessed are you among women,
and blessed is the fruit of your womb.
And how does this happen to me,
that the mother of my Lord should come to me?
For at the moment the sound of your greeting
reached my ears,
the infant in my womb leaped for joy.
Blessed are you who believed
that what was spoken to you by the Lord
would be fulfilled."

The Gospel of the Lord.

EXPLANATION OF THE READING

Mary receives the message of the angel, and, unlike Zechariah, she cannot
be silent: she must share her joy. When she greets Elizabeth, several
things happen at once. Elizabeth is filled with the Holy Spirit, and suddenly
and mysteriously she understands who Mary is, "blessed among women."
At the same time, the infant John the Baptist leaps in her womb, and
Elizabeth recognizes that, blessed as Mary is, the child in her womb is
more blessed still. Mary is blessed not because she carries the Christ in
her womb, but because she "believed." We are all called to be like Mary.

CHRISTMAS

December 25, 2009

SOLEMNITY OF THE NATIVITY OF THE LORD

A reading from the holy Gospel according to Luke

Luke 2:1–14

In those days a decree went out from
    Caesar Augustus
  that the whole world should be enrolled.
This was the first enrollment,
  when Quirinius was governor of Syria.
So all went to be enrolled, each to his own town.
And Joseph too went up from Galilee from the town
    of Nazareth
  to Judea, to the city of David that is called
    Bethlehem,
  because he was of the house and family of David,
  to be enrolled with Mary, his betrothed,
    who was with child.
While they were there,
  the time came for her to have her child,
  and she gave birth to her firstborn son.

She wrapped him in swaddling clothes and laid him
    in a manger,
    because there was no room for them in the inn.

Now there were shepherds in that region living
    in the fields
    and keeping the night watch over their flock.
The angel of the Lord appeared to them
    and the glory of the Lord shone around them,
    and they were struck with great fear.
The angel said to them,
    "Do not be afraid;
    for behold, I proclaim to you good news of great joy
    that will be for all the people.
For today in the city of David
    a savior has been born for you who is Christ
        and Lord.
And this will be a sign for you:
    you will find an infant wrapped in swaddling clothes
    and lying in a manger."
And suddenly there was a multitude of
    the heavenly host with the angel,
    praising God and saying:
        "Glory to God in the highest
            and on earth peace to those on whom
            his favor rests."

The Gospel of the Lord.

Luke recounts Mary's delivery of her child in poverty and its proclamation to poor shepherds. Today do we dare seek the Lord in the place among those whom he chose to be born? May we be more and more open to what God's poor ones wish to teach us.

December 27, 2009

FEAST OF THE HOLY FAMILY OF JESUS, MARY, AND JOSEPH

A reading from the holy Gospel according to Luke
2:41–52

Each year Jesus' parents·went to Jerusalem for the
    feast of Passover,
  and when he was twelve years old,
  they went up according to festival custom.
After they had completed its days,
    as they were returning,
  the boy Jesus remained behind in Jerusalem,
  but his parents did not know it.
Thinking that he was in the caravan,
  they journeyed for a day
  and looked for him among their relatives and
    acquaintances,
  but not finding him,
  they returned to Jerusalem to look for him.
After three days they found him in the temple,
  sitting in the midst of the teachers,
  listening to them and asking them questions,

and all who heard him were astounded
at his understanding and his answers.
When his parents saw him,
they were astonished,
and his mother said to him,
"Son, why have you done this to us?
Your father and I have been looking for you with
great anxiety."
And he said to them,
"Why were you looking for me?
Did you not know that I must be in
my Father's house?"
But they did not understand what he said to them.
He went down with them and came to Nazareth,
and was obedient to them;
and his mother kept all these things in her heart.
And Jesus advanced in wisdom and age and favor
before God and man.

The Gospel of the Lord.

EXPLANATION OF THE READING

We meditate on this story of the finding in the temple every time we pray
the joyful mysteries of the Rosary. But in some ways, this story is anything
but joyful. Imagine the feelings of Mary and Joseph when they first
realized Jesus was not with them. And then imagine what they must have
felt after looking for him for three days. No wonder Mary says, "why have
you done this to us?" The story of the finding in the temple reminds us
that family life is not easy, nor is it supposed to be. A family's goal is not
to avoid trials and difficulties, but rather to confront them with God's
grace, as Mary, Joseph, and Jesus did. In this encounter, Mary and Joseph
learn something about their son. And Jesus the teacher "came to
Nazareth, and was obedient to them."

January 1, 2010

Solemnity of the Blessed Virgin Mary, Mother of God

The Octave Day of Christmas

A reading from the holy Gospel according to Luke

2:16–21

The shepherds went in haste to Bethlehem and found
    Mary and Joseph,
  and the infant lying in the manger.
When they saw this,
  they made known the message
  that had been told them about this child.
All who heard it were amazed
  by what had been told them by the shepherds.
And Mary kept all these things,
  reflecting on them in her heart.
Then the shepherds returned,
  glorifying and praising God
  for all they had heard and seen,
  just as it had been told to them.

When eight days were completed for his circumcision,
  he was named Jesus, the name given him by
    the angel
  before he was conceived in the womb.

The Gospel of the Lord.

EXPLANATION OF THE READING

In 1968, Pope Paul VI declared this day the World Day of Prayer for Peace. Peace, he insisted, is not just a dream; it is a duty. As we stand at the threshold of this new year, can we see possibilities for peace in our families, our local communities, and our world? Or are we so disillusioned by past failures that all we can see is more discord, more violence, more war? On this first day of a new year, let us ask the intercession of Mary, Queen of Peace, that our hearts may be filled with hope for the future.

January 3, 2010

SOLEMNITY OF THE EPIPHANY OF THE LORD

A reading from the holy Gospel according to Matthew

2:1–12

When Jesus was born in Bethlehem of Judea,
   in the days of King Herod,
   behold, magi from the east arrived in Jerusalem,
     saying,
   "Where is the newborn king of the Jews?
We saw his star at its rising
   and have come to do him homage."
When King Herod heard this,
   he was greatly troubled,
   and all Jerusalem with him.
Assembling all the chief priests and the scribes
     of the people,
   he inquired of them where the Christ was to be born.
They said to him, "In Bethlehem of Judea,
   for thus it has been written through the prophet:

And you, Bethlehem, land of Judah,
  are by no means least among the rulers of Judah;
since from you shall come a ruler,
  who is to shepherd my people Israel."
Then Herod called the magi secretly
  and ascertained from them the time of
    the star's appearance.
He sent them to Bethlehem and said,
  "Go and search diligently for the child.
When you have found him, bring me word,
  that I too may go and do him homage."
After their audience with the king they set out.
And behold, the star that they had seen at its rising
    preceded them,
  until it came and stopped over the place where
    the child was.
They were overjoyed at seeing the star,
  and on entering the house
  they saw the child with Mary his mother.
They prostrated themselves and did him homage.
Then they opened their treasures
  and offered him gifts of gold, frankincense,
    and myrrh.
And having been warned in a dream not to return
    to Herod,
  they departed for their country by another way.

The Gospel of the Lord.

EXPLANATION OF THE READING

The word *epiphany* means "showing forth" or "manifestation." We don't know much about the magi, the "wise men," to whom tradition has assigned names and stories as colorful as their costumes. But we do know two very important things about them. We know they came "from the east." They were not of the chosen people, but foreigners, Gentiles. And we know that they were "overjoyed" at where the star led them, that they acknowledged Jesus as king and God. From the first moments of his life, Jesus breaks through the boundaries that we human beings set up to separate ourselves from one another. When it comes to God's love, there are no outsiders.

January 10, 2010

FEAST OF THE BAPTISM OF THE LORD

A reading from the holy Gospel according to Luke   3:15–16, 21–22

The people were filled with expectation,
  and all were asking in their hearts
  whether John might be the Christ.
John answered them all, saying,
  "I am baptizing you with water,
  but one mightier than I is coming.
I am not worthy to loosen the thongs of his sandals.
He will baptize you with the Holy Spirit and fire."

After all the people had been baptized
  and Jesus also had been baptized and was praying,
  heaven was opened and the Holy Spirit descended
    upon him
  in bodily form like a dove.

And a voice came from heaven,
  "You are my beloved Son;
  with you I am well pleased."

The Gospel of the Lord.

EXPLANATION OF THE READING

As we celebrate the Baptism of Jesus, we are reminded of our own
Baptism into the Church. For most of us, the choice to be baptized was
made by our parents. Therefore, God calls us, especially, on this last day
of the Christmas season, to renew our commitment to reject Satan and
sin, claim God as Father, proclaim Jesus Christ as Lord, believe in the Holy
Spirit, and accept the tenets of the Catholic faith. Just as we were baptized
with the water of everlasting life, so too must we be water and fire for
those who thirst and long for life.

ORDINARY TIME DURING WINTER

SECOND SUNDAY IN ORDINARY TIME

A reading from the holy Gospel according to John

2:1–11

There was a wedding at Cana in Galilee,
  and the mother of Jesus was there.
Jesus and his disciples were also invited to
    the wedding.
When the wine ran short,
  the mother of Jesus said to him,
  "They have no wine."
And Jesus said to her,
  "Woman, how does your concern affect me?
My hour has not yet come."
His mother said to the servers,
  "Do whatever he tells you."
Now there were six stone water jars there for
    Jewish ceremonial washings,
  each holding twenty to thirty gallons.
Jesus told them,
  "Fill the jars with water."

So they filled them to the brim.
Then he told them,
  "Draw some out now and take it to the headwaiter."
So they took it.
And when the headwaiter tasted the water that
    had become wine,
  without knowing where it came from
  —although the servers who had drawn
    the water knew—,
  the headwaiter called the bridegroom and said
    to him,
  "Everyone serves good wine first,
  and then when people have drunk freely,
    an inferior one;
  but you have kept the good wine until now."
Jesus did this as the beginning of his signs at Cana
    in Galilee
  and so revealed his glory,
  and his disciples began to believe in him.

The Gospel of the Lord.

EXPLANATION OF THE READING

The wonderful story of the wedding at Cana gives us a glimpse into the
compassion of Jesus and his mother. Jesus has an incredible mission to
fulfill—yet he takes time to come to a wedding. Mary, seeing the wine
running out, is concerned for the young couple, and she does not hesitate
to approach Jesus on their behalf. And Jesus responds with a gesture that
reflects the superabundant generosity and love of God. Jesus is with us not
only in our sorrows, but in our joys. And Mary, his watchful mother, is
ready to intercede for us.

January 24, 2010

Third Sunday in Ordinary Time

A reading from the holy Gospel according to Luke

1:1–4; 4:14–21

Since many have undertaken to compile
    a narrative of the events
that have been fulfilled among us,
just as those who were eyewitnesses from
    the beginning
and ministers of the word have handed them down
    to us,
I too have decided,
after investigating everything accurately anew,
to write it down in an orderly sequence for you,
most excellent Theophilus,
so that you may realize the certainty of
    the teachings
you have received.

Jesus returned to Galilee in the power of the Spirit,
    and news of him spread throughout
        the whole region.
He taught in their synagogues and was praised by all.
He came to Nazareth, where he had grown up,
    and went according to his custom
    into the synagogue on the sabbath day.
He stood up to read and was handed a scroll of the
    prophet Isaiah.

He unrolled the scroll and found the passage where it
was written:
The Spirit of the Lord is upon me,
because he has anointed me
to bring glad tidings to the poor.
He has sent me to proclaim liberty to captives
and recovery of sight to the blind,
to let the oppressed go free,
and to proclaim a year acceptable to the Lord.
Rolling up the scroll, he handed it back to the
attendant and sat down,
and the eyes of all in the synagogue looked intently
at him.
He said to them,
"Today this Scripture passage is fulfilled in your
hearing."

The Gospel of the Lord.

EXPLANATION OF THE READING

At his home synagogue at Nazareth, Jesus proclaims the coming of God's
kingdom, in the words of the prophet Isaiah. A new era has begun, "a year
acceptable to the Lord." It is a topsy-turvy world. Good News is proclaimed
to the poor, prisoners are released from bondage, the blind have their
sight restored, and the oppressed are set free. All those whom our world
considers as counting for nothing suddenly count for everything. Jesus'
words in the synagogue at Nazareth make it clear that God's kingdom
will be unlike any other kingdom. It is not that rich and poor are equal
in God's kingdom. Rather, there is a preferential option for the poor, the
oppressed, and the lowly.

January 31, 2010

FOURTH SUNDAY IN ORDINARY TIME

A reading from the holy Gospel according to Luke
4:21–30

Jesus began speaking in the synagogue, saying:
  "Today this Scripture passage is fulfilled in
    your hearing."
And all spoke highly of him
  and were amazed at the gracious words that
    came from his mouth.
They also asked, "Isn't this the son of Joseph?"
He said to them, "Surely you will quote me
    this proverb,
  'Physician, cure yourself,' and say,
  'Do here in your native place
  the things that we heard were done in Capernaum.'"
And he said, "Amen, I say to you,
  no prophet is accepted in his own native place.
Indeed, I tell you,
  there were many widows in Israel in the days
    of Elijah
  when the sky was closed for three and a half years
  and a severe famine spread over the entire land.
It was to none of these that Elijah was sent,
  but only to a widow in Zarephath in the land
    of Sidon.
Again, there were many lepers in Israel
  during the time of Elisha the prophet;

yet not one of them was cleansed, but only
    Naaman the Syrian."
When the people in the synagogue heard this,
    they were all filled with fury.
They rose up, drove him out of the town,
    and led him to the brow of the hill
    on which their town had been built,
    to hurl him down headlong.
But Jesus passed through the midst of them and
    went away.

The Gospel of the Lord.

EXPLANATION OF THE READING

Jesus has made a tremendous impression on the people. But even as all
speak highly of him, and are "amazed" at his words, darkness and doubt
begin to creep in. Isn't this Jesus, the son of Joseph the carpenter, some
ask? So how did he come by this amazing wisdom? And how is he able to
work such mighty deeds? Paradoxically, it is because they think they
know who Jesus is that the people of Nazareth are unable to accept him,
and they even attempt to take his life. From the very beginning of his
ministry, Jesus knows that he will suffer the fate of the prophets who have
gone before him. Are we who followed Jesus prepared to encounter that
same misunderstanding—perhaps from those we love the best?

February 7, 2010

FIFTH SUNDAY IN ORDINARY TIME

A reading from the holy Gospel according to Luke 5:1–11

While the crowd was pressing in on Jesus and
     listening to the word of God,
  he was standing by the Lake of Gennesaret.
He saw two boats there alongside the lake;
  the fishermen had disembarked and were washing
     their nets.
Getting into one of the boats, the one belonging
     to Simon,
  he asked him to put out a short distance from
     the shore.
Then he sat down and taught the crowds from
     the boat.
After he had finished speaking, he said to Simon,
  "Put out into deep water and lower your nets for
     a catch."
Simon said in reply,
  "Master, we have worked hard all night and have
     caught nothing,
  but at your command I will lower the nets."
When they had done this, they caught a great number
     of fish
  and their nets were tearing.
They signaled to their partners in the other boat
  to come to help them.

They came and filled both boats
so that the boats were in danger of sinking.
When Simon Peter saw this, he fell at the knees of
Jesus and said,
"Depart from me, Lord, for I am a sinful man."
For astonishment at the catch of fish they had made
seized him
and all those with him,
and likewise James and John, the sons of Zebedee,
who were partners of Simon.
Jesus said to Simon, "Do not be afraid;
from now on you will be catching men."
When they brought their boats to the shore,
they left everything and followed him.

The Gospel of the Lord.

EXPLANATION OF THE READING

There is already a connection, perhaps even a friendship, between Simon Peter and Jesus. Peter lets Jesus use his boat to preach to the crowds gathered on the shore. And at Jesus' command to "put out into deep water," Peter obeys, even though it seems unlikely that they will catch anything. But when the nets come back so full that the boats are in danger of sinking, Peter recognizes something of who Jesus is. He calls him "Lord," and suddenly he becomes acutely aware of his own sinfulness. But Jesus tells him not to fear, and calls him to follow. To be a follower of Jesus is to "put out into deep water" day by day. Sometimes we feel we are in over our heads. But Jesus is always there with words of reassurance: "Do not be afraid."

February 14, 2010

Sixth Sunday in Ordinary Time

A reading from the holy Gospel according to Luke
6:17, 20–26

Jesus came down with the Twelve
and stood on a stretch of level ground
with a great crowd of his disciples
and a large number of the people
from all Judea and Jerusalem
and the coastal region of Tyre and Sidon.
And raising his eyes toward his disciples he said:
"Blessed are you who are poor,
for the kingdom of God is yours.
Blessed are you who are now hungry,
for you will be satisfied.
Blessed are you who are now weeping,
for you will laugh.
Blessed are you when people hate you,
and when they exclude and insult you,
and denounce your name as evil
on account of the Son of Man.
Rejoice and leap for joy on that day!
Behold, your reward will be great in heaven.
For their ancestors treated the prophets in
the same way.
But woe to you who are rich,
for you have received your consolation.

Woe to you who are filled now,
   for you will be hungry.
Woe to you who laugh now,
   for you will grieve and weep.
Woe to you when all speak well of you,
   for their ancestors treated the false prophets in
      this way."

The Gospel of the Lord.

EXPLANATION OF THE READING

The Beatitudes should unsettle us, because they turn our world upside down. Jesus showers blessings on exactly those people whom the world considers to be cursed—the poor, the hungry, those who weep, those who are hated, excluded, and insulted. And he heaps woes upon those whom our world considers to be blessed: the rich, those with plenty to eat, those who laugh, those who are spoken well of by others. In our Church, our world, our communities, and our families, we need to cultivate "Beatitude attitudes." We need to see in the afflicted of the world more than objects for charity. Rather, we need to see them as beloved, chosen, blessed by God.

LENT

FIRST SUNDAY OF LENT

A reading from the holy Gospel according to Luke
4:1–13

Filled with the Holy Spirit, Jesus returned from
the Jordan
and was led by the Spirit into the desert for
forty days,
to be tempted by the devil.
He ate nothing during those days,
and when they were over he was hungry.
The devil said to him,
"If you are the Son of God,
command this stone to become bread."
Jesus answered him,
"It is written, *One does not live on bread alone.*"
Then he took him up and showed him
all the kingdoms of the world in a single instant.
The devil said to him,
"I shall give to you all this power and glory;
for it has been handed over to me,
and I may give it to whomever I wish.
All this will be yours, if you worship me."

Jesus said to him in reply,
"It is written:
You shall worship the Lord, your God,
and him alone shall you serve."
Then he led him to Jerusalem,
made him stand on the parapet of the temple,
and said to him,
"If you are the Son of God,
throw yourself down from here, for it is written:
He will command his angels concerning you,
to guard you,
and:
With their hands they will support you,
lest you dash your foot against a stone."
Jesus said to him in reply,
"It also says,
You shall not put the Lord, your God, to the test."
When the devil had finished every temptation,
he departed from him for a time.

The Gospel of the Lord.

EXPLANATION OF THE READING

Jesus has been fasting in the desert for 40 days; he is tired and hungry. That is precisely when the devil strikes. Prove you are the Son of God, he says. Seize power; take control. It is the same for us. Temptation comes when we are worn down, when our defenses are lowered. But we can find the courage to resist in the inspired word of God, just as Jesus does. Jesus does not get involved in circuitous arguments with the devil; instead, he defeats him with God's holy word.

February 28, 2010

Second Sunday of Lent

A reading from the holy Gospel according to Luke

9:28b–36

Jesus took Peter, John, and James
and went up the mountain to pray.
While he was praying, his face changed in appearance
and his clothing became dazzling white.
And behold, two men were conversing with him,
Moses and Elijah,
who appeared in glory and spoke of his exodus
that he was going to accomplish in Jerusalem.
Peter and his companions had been overcome
by sleep,
but becoming fully awake,
they saw his glory and the two men standing
with him.
As they were about to part from him,
Peter said to Jesus,
"Master, it is good that we are here;
let us make three tents,
one for you, one for Moses, and one for Elijah."
But he did not know what he was saying.
While he was still speaking,
a cloud came and cast a shadow over them,
and they became frightened when they entered
the cloud.

Then from the cloud came a voice that said,
  "This is my chosen Son; listen to him."
After the voice had spoken, Jesus was found alone.
They fell silent and did not at that time
  tell anyone what they had seen.

The Gospel of the Lord.

EXPLANATION OF THE READING

The account of the Transfiguration of the Lord is proclaimed every year on the Second Sunday of Lent, giving us a glimpse into the glorious destiny that awaits the faithful followers of Christ. The custom of reading today's Gospel near the beginning of Lent may come from an ancient tradition that held that the Transfiguration took place 40 days before Good Friday. Moses and Elijah, who appear at the side of Jesus, also prepared for their life's work with a 40-day fast and a 40-day sojourn.

    In Luke's presentation of the transfiguration, Moses and Elijah converse with Jesus, concerning the exodus that he is about to accomplish in Jerusalem, and a voice from heaven declares Jesus to be God's beloved Son. The cross, a symbol of sin, defect, suffering, and death, will be transformed into a symbol of holiness, victory, exaltation, and life, for by it the beloved Son leads us out of death into life. As we walk the way of the cross, may the Holy Spirit sustain us in an awareness of this truth.

March 7, 2010

THIRD SUNDAY OF LENT

A reading from the holy Gospel according to Luke

13:1–9

Some people told Jesus about the Galileans
  whose blood Pilate had mingled with the blood of
    their sacrifices.

Jesus said to them in reply,
    "Do you think that because these Galileans
        suffered in this way
    they were greater sinners than all other Galileans?
By no means!
But I tell you, if you do not repent,
    you will all perish as they did!
Or those eighteen people who were killed
    when the tower at Siloam fell on them—
    do you think they were more guilty
    than everyone else who lived in Jerusalem?
By no means!
But I tell you, if you do not repent,
    you will all perish as they did!"

And he told them this parable:
    "There once was a person who had a fig tree
        planted in his orchard,
    and when he came in search of fruit on it but
        found none,
    he said to the gardener,
    'For three years now I have come in search of fruit
        on this fig tree
    but have found none.
So cut it down.
Why should it exhaust the soil?'
He said to him in reply,
    'Sir, leave it for this year also,

and I shall cultivate the ground around it and
    fertilize it;
  it may bear fruit in the future.
If not you can cut it down.'"

The Gospel of the Lord.

EXPLANATION OF THE READING

In Luke's account of the Gospel, Jesus counters the common belief that
suffering is the measure of punishment deserved. Disasters do not invade
our lives as divine retribution for sin, yet disasters do remind us of life's
frailty and of our need to remain in right relationship with God. The Lord's
patience with us, the gift of time, provides opportunities for us to bear
good fruit.

March 14, 2010

FOURTH SUNDAY OF LENT

A reading from the holy Gospel according to Luke
15:1–3, 11–32

Tax collectors and sinners were all drawing near to
    listen to Jesus,
  but the Pharisees and scribes began to complain,
    saying,
  "This man welcomes sinners and eats with them."
So to them Jesus addressed this parable:
"A man had two sons, and the younger son said to
    his father,
  'Father give me the share of your estate that should
    come to me.'

So the father divided the property between them.
After a few days, the younger son collected all his
    belongings
  and set off to a distant country
  where he squandered his inheritance on a life of
    dissipation.
When he had freely spent everything,
  a severe famine struck that country,
  and he found himself in dire need.
So he hired himself out to one of the local citizens
  who sent him to his farm to tend the swine.
And he longed to eat his fill of the pods on which
    the swine fed,
  but nobody gave him any.
Coming to his senses he thought,
  'How many of my father's hired workers
  have more than enough food to eat,
  but here am I, dying from hunger.
I shall get up and go to my father and I shall say
    to him,
  "Father, I have sinned against heaven and
    against you.
I no longer deserve to be called your son;
  treat me as you would treat one of your
    hired workers."'
So he got up and went back to his father.
While he was still a long way off,
  his father caught sight of him, and was filled
    with compassion.

He ran to his son, embraced him and kissed him.
His son said to him,
  'Father, I have sinned against heaven and
    against you;
  I no longer deserve to be called your son.'
But his father ordered his servants,
  'Quickly bring the finest robe and put it on him;
  put a ring on his finger and sandals on his feet.
Take the fattened calf and slaughter it.
Then let us celebrate with a feast,
  because this son of mine was dead, and has come
    to life again;
  he was lost, and has been found.'
Then the celebration began.
Now the older son had been out in the field
  and, on his way back, as he neared the house,
  he heard the sound of music and dancing.
He called one of the servants and asked what this
    might mean.
The servant said to him,
  'Your brother has returned
  and your father has slaughtered the fattened calf
  because he has him back safe and sound.'
He became angry,
  and when he refused to enter the house,
  his father came out and pleaded with him.
He said to his father in reply,
  'Look, all these years I served you
  and not once did I disobey your orders;

yet you never gave me even a young goat to
  feast on with my friends.
But when your son returns
  who swallowed up your property with prostitutes,
  for him you slaughter the fattened calf.'
He said to him,
  'My son, you are here with me always;
  everything I have is yours.
But now we must celebrate and rejoice,
  because your brother was dead and has come to
    life again;
  he was lost and has been found.'"

The Gospel of the Lord.

EXPLANATION OF THE READING

Today is known as *Laetare* Sunday, a day that marks the halfway point
of Lent and that celebrates our joy in being that much closer to the
Resurrection of Christ, the day of our salvation. The name of the day
comes from the first word of today's Entrance Antiphon from Mass,
"Rejoice, Jerusalem!"

In the Gospel, we hear the parable of the prodigal son. We know only
of the decision of the younger son, who accepts the fullness of the father's
embrace. The elder "faithful" son, filled with resentment at the father's
lavish forgiveness of his brother, remains in the field. We are not told
whether the father's message of extravagant love for both sons will move
him to enter into the celebration of eternal life. In this holy season,
whether we are distant or close to home, we are invited to fuller life.

March 21, 2010

FIFTH SUNDAY OF LENT

A reading from the holy Gospel according to John

8:1–11

Jesus went to the Mount of Olives.
But early in the morning he arrived again in
    the temple area,
  and all the people started coming to him,
  and he sat down and taught them.
Then the scribes and the Pharisees brought a woman
  who had been caught in adultery
  and made her stand in the middle.
They said to him,
  "Teacher, this woman was caught
  in the very act of committing adultery.
Now in the law, Moses commanded us to stone
    such women.
So what do you say?"
They said this to test him,
  so that they could have some charge to bring
    against him.
Jesus bent down and began to write on the ground
    with his finger.
But when they continued asking him,
  he straightened up and said to them,
  "Let the one among you who is without sin
  be the first to throw a stone at her."
Again he bent down and wrote on the ground.

And in response, they went away one by one,
   beginning with the elders.
So he was left alone with the woman before him.
Then Jesus straightened up and said to her,
   "Woman, where are they?
Has no one condemned you?"
She replied, "No one, sir."
Then Jesus said, "Neither do I condemn you.
Go, and from now on do not sin any more."

The Gospel of the Lord.

EXPLANATION OF THE READING

The adulterous woman's execution was thwarted by the dropping of
stones, and not by her protestations of repentance. Her accusers laid
down their stones and their hearts of stone as Jesus' penetrating challenge
enabled them to make an honest assessment of their own lives. The
woman herself made no protestation of a repentant life, but acknowledged
that her accusers had departed. Jesus, while siding with those who refuse
to stone her, challenges her to a new life free from this sin.

March 28, 2010

PALM SUNDAY OF THE LORD'S PASSION

The Passion of our Lord Jesus Christ according to Luke   23:1–49

The elders of the people, chief priests and scribes,
   arose and brought Jesus before Pilate.
They brought charges against him, saying,
   "We found this man misleading our people;

he opposes the payment of taxes to Caesar
and maintains that he is the Christ, a king."
Pilate asked him, "Are you the king of the Jews?"
He said to him in reply, "You say so."
Pilate then addressed the chief priests and the crowds,
"I find this man not guilty."
But they were adamant and said,
"He is inciting the people with his teaching
throughout all Judea,
from Galilee where he began even to here."

On hearing this Pilate asked if the man was a
Galilean;
and upon learning that he was under Herod's
jurisdiction,
he sent him to Herod who was in Jerusalem
at that time.
Herod was very glad to see Jesus;
he had been wanting to see him for a long time,
for he had heard about him
and had been hoping to see him perform some sign.
He questioned him at length,
but he gave him no answer.
The chief priests and scribes, meanwhile,
stood by accusing him harshly.
Herod and his soldiers treated him contemptuously
and mocked him,
and after clothing him in resplendent garb,
he sent him back to Pilate.

Herod and Pilate became friends that very day,
  even though they had been enemies formerly.
Pilate then summoned the chief priests, the rulers,
    and the people
  and said to them, "You brought this man to me
  and accused him of inciting the people to revolt.
I have conducted my investigation in your presence
  and have not found this man guilty
  of the charges you have brought against him,
  nor did Herod, for he sent him back to us.
So no capital crime has been committed by him.
Therefore I shall have him flogged and then
    release him."

But all together they shouted out,
  "Away with this man!
  Release Barabbas to us."
—Now Barabbas had been imprisoned for a rebellion
  that had taken place in the city and for murder.—
Again Pilate addressed them, still wishing to
    release Jesus,
  but they continued their shouting,
  "Crucify him! Crucify him!"
Pilate addressed them a third time,
  "What evil has this man done?
  I found him guilty of no capital crime.
Therefore I shall have him flogged and then
    release him."

With loud shouts, however,
   they persisted in calling for his crucifixion,
   and their voices prevailed.
The verdict of Pilate was that their demand should
      be granted.
So he released the man who had been imprisoned
   for rebellion and murder, for whom they asked,
   and he handed Jesus over to them to deal with
      as they wished.

As they led him away
   they took hold of a certain Simon, a Cyrenian,
   who was coming in from the country;
   and after laying the cross on him,
   they made him carry it behind Jesus.
A large crowd of people followed Jesus,
   including many women who mourned and
      lamented him.
Jesus turned to them and said,
   "Daughters of Jerusalem, do not weep for me;
   weep instead for yourselves and for your children
   for indeed, the days are coming when people
      will say,
   'Blessed are the barren,
   the wombs that never bore
   and the breasts that never nursed.'
At that time people will say to the mountains,
   'Fall upon us!'
   and to the hills, 'Cover us!'

for if these things are done when the wood is green
   what will happen when it is dry?"
Now two others, both criminals,
   were led away with him to be executed.

When they came to the place called the Skull,
   they crucified him and the criminals there,
   one on his right, the other on his left.
Then Jesus said,
   "Father, forgive them, they know not what they do."
They divided his garments by casting lots.
The people stood by and watched;
   the rulers, meanwhile, sneered at him and said,
   "He saved others, let him save himself
   if he is the chosen one, the Christ of God."
Even the soldiers jeered at him.
As they approached to offer him wine they called out,
   "If you are King of the Jews, save yourself."
Above him there was an inscription that read,
   "This is the King of the Jews."

Now one of the criminals hanging there reviled Jesus,
      saying,
   "Are you not the Christ?
   Save yourself and us."
The other, however, rebuking him, said in reply,
   "Have you no fear of God,
   for you are subject to the same condemnation?

And indeed, we have been condemned justly,
for the sentence we received corresponds to
our crimes,
but this man has done nothing criminal."
Then he said,
"Jesus, remember me when you come into
your kingdom."
He replied to him,
"Amen, I say to you,
today you will be with me in Paradise."

It was now about noon and darkness came over
the whole land
until three in the afternoon
because of an eclipse of the sun.
Then the veil of the temple was torn down the middle.
Jesus cried out in a loud voice,
"Father, into your hands I commend my spirit";
and when he had said this he breathed his last.

Here all kneel and pause for a short time.

The centurion who witnessed what had happened
glorified God and said,
"This man was innocent beyond doubt."
When all the people who had gathered for this
spectacle saw what had happened,
they returned home beating their breasts;
but all his acquaintances stood at a distance,

including the women who had followed him
   from Galilee
and saw these events.

The Gospel of the Lord.

Longer form: Luke 22:14—23:56

EXPLANATION OF THE READING

Today's celebration has been known by several names through its long history. It has been called "Palm Sunday," and it has been called "Passion Sunday." Today, it is called "Palm Sunday of the Lord's Passion," a title which reflects the dual nature of this day, the great beginning of Holy Week. Our liturgy begins with the joyful waving of palm branches, proclaiming Jesus the Messiah as he rides humbly into Jerusalem. But it continues with the reading of the Passion according to Luke, when the same crowds who welcomed Jesus with joy assent to his torture and crucifixion. Our joyful entrance into Jerusalem becomes the way of the cross.

EASTER

April 4, 2010

EASTER SUNDAY: SOLEMNITY OF THE RESURRECTION OF THE LORD

A reading from the holy Gospel according to John

20:1–9

On the first day of the week,
   Mary of Magdala came to the tomb early in
      the morning,
   while it was still dark,
   and saw the stone removed from the tomb.
So she ran and went to Simon Peter
   and to the other disciple whom Jesus loved,
      and told them,
   "They have taken the Lord from the tomb,
   and we don't know where they put him."
So Peter and the other disciple went out and came
      to the tomb.
They both ran, but the other disciple ran faster
      than Peter
   and arrived at the tomb first;
   he bent down and saw the burial cloths there,
      but did not go in.

When Simon Peter arrived after him,
   he went into the tomb and saw
      the burial cloths there,
   and the cloth that had covered his head,
   not with the burial cloths but rolled up in
      a separate place.
Then the other disciple also went in,
   the one who had arrived at the tomb first,
   and he saw and believed.
For they did not yet understand the Scripture
   that he had to rise from the dead.

The Gospel of the Lord.

EXPLANATION OF THE READING

Came, saw, ran, went: the Gospel accounts of the Resurrection are full
of movement and action. Christ's rising from the dead set in motion an
unstoppable chain of events, as the faithful women, then the disciples,
and (little by little) the whole world are set running by the glorious news
that Christ is risen. "There is an upward movement in the whole of
creation," wrote St. Maximus of Turin in an Easter homily, "each element
raising itself to something higher. . . . In one and the same movement, our
Savior's passion raises men from the depths, lifts them up from the earth,
and sets them in the heights." The Good News should get us moving, too.

April 11, 2010

SECOND SUNDAY OF EASTER/ DIVINE MERCY SUNDAY

A reading from the holy Gospel according to John

20:19–31

On the evening of that first day of the week,
  when the doors were locked, where the
    disciples were,
  for fear of the Jews,
  Jesus came and stood in their midst
  and said to them, "Peace be with you."
When he had said this, he showed them his hands
    and his side.
The disciples rejoiced when they saw the Lord.
Jesus said to them again, "Peace be with you.
As the Father has sent me, so I send you."
And when he had said this, he breathed on them and
    said to them,
  "Receive the Holy Spirit.
Whose sins you forgive are forgiven them,
  and whose sins you retain are retained."

Thomas, called Didymus, one of the Twelve,
  was not with them when Jesus came.
So the other disciples said to him, "We have seen
    the Lord."
But he said to them,
  "Unless I see the mark of the nails in his hands

and put my finger into the nailmarks
and put my hand into his side, I will not believe."

Now a week later his disciples were again inside
and Thomas was with them.
Jesus came, although the doors were locked,
and stood in their midst and said,
"Peace be with you."
Then he said to Thomas, "Put your finger here and
see my hands,
and bring your hand and put it into my side,
and do not be unbelieving, but believe."
Thomas answered and said to him, "My Lord and
my God!"
Jesus said to him, "Have you come to believe because
you have seen me?
Blessed are those who have not seen and
have believed."

Now Jesus did many other signs in the presence of
his disciples
that are not written in this book.
But these are written that you may come to believe
that Jesus is the Christ, the Son of God,
and that through this belief you may have life in
his name.

The Gospel of the Lord.

EXPLANATION OF THE READING

For the Church, the week after Easter is a time of grace and joy, a time when we feel especially close to the risen Lord; a time when our churches and the world around us seem fragrant. But for Thomas that first week after Easter must have been the darkest of his life. His Lord had been crucified, but his friends are not even grieving: instead, they are rejoicing, for, they tell him, Jesus has risen from the dead. But Thomas cannot believe. Not until Jesus comes to meet him, and shows him his wounds, does grief give way to joy and faith for Thomas. Jesus reaches every disciple in a different way; but to all he gives the needed grace to be able to say, with Thomas, "my Lord and my God."

April 18, 2010

THIRD SUNDAY OF EASTER

A reading from the holy Gospel according to John
21:1–14

At that time, Jesus revealed himself to his disciples at
    the Sea of Tiberias.
He revealed himself in this way.
Together were Simon Peter, Thomas called Didymus,
    Nathanael from Cana in Galilee,
    Zebedee's sons, and two others of his disciples.
Simon Peter said to them, "I am going fishing."
They said to him, "We also will come with you."
So they went out and got into the boat,
    but that night they caught nothing.
When it was already dawn, Jesus was standing
    on the shore;
    but the disciples did not realize that it was Jesus.

Jesus said to them, "Children, have you caught
    anything to eat?"
They answered him, "No."
So he said to them, "Cast the net over the right side
    of the boat
    and you will find something."
So they cast it, and were not able to pull it in
    because of the number of fish.
So the disciple whom Jesus loved said to Peter,
    "It is the Lord."
When Simon Peter heard that it was the Lord,
    he tucked in his garment, for he was lightly clad,
    and jumped into the sea.
The other disciples came in the boat,
    for they were not far from shore, only about
        a hundred yards,
    dragging the net with the fish.
When they climbed out on shore,
    they saw a charcoal fire with fish on it and bread.
Jesus said to them, "Bring some of the fish you
    just caught."
So Simon Peter went over and dragged the net ashore
    full of one hundred fifty-three large fish.
Even though there were so many, the net was not torn.
Jesus said to them, "Come, have breakfast."
And none of the disciples dared to ask him,
    "Who are you?"
    because they realized it was the Lord.

Jesus came over and took the bread and gave it
    to them,
  and in like manner the fish.
This was now the third time Jesus was revealed to
    his disciples
  after being raised from the dead.

The Gospel of the Lord.

Longer form: John 21:1–19

EXPLANATION OF THE READING

After the miraculous catch of fishes, the disciples come to shore. Jesus
is there—the risen Lord, the God of all—and yet he humbly serves them
bread and fish, which, it seems, he has prepared for them himself. Again
and again in the Gospel according to John, a great sign—the feeding of
a multitude, a miraculous catch—is accompanied by humble service. As
we seek the vision that will help us to see the presence of the risen Christ
in the world around us, there is one thing we can be sure of: we will find
him serving his people.

April 25, 2010

FOURTH SUNDAY OF EASTER

A reading from the holy Gospel
according to John   *10:27–30*

Jesus said:
"My sheep hear my voice;
  I know them, and they follow me.
I give them eternal life, and they shall never perish.
No one can take them out of my hand.

My Father, who has given them to me, is greater
    than all,
    and no one can take them out of the Father's hand.
The Father and I are one."

The Gospel of the Lord.

EXPLANATION OF THE READING

This Fourth Sunday of Easter is also known as Good Shepherd Sunday.
During this week, we might take time to meditate on the words of Psalm 23,
a prayer Jesus knew and loved. The prayer begins with a vivid picture of
God as shepherd, caring for our wants, guiding us to a place of rest, peace,
and abundance. Psalm 23 not only tells us what God is like — a caring
shepherd — it also tells us how we should view ourselves. We are sheep,
not shepherds; therefore we should seek to be simple and humble,
following the voice of our shepherd and trusting absolutely in his ability,
and desire, to provide for us.

May 2, 2010

FIFTH SUNDAY OF EASTER

A reading from the holy Gospel
according to John
13:31–33a, 34–35

When Judas had left them, Jesus said,
    "Now is the Son of Man glorified, and God is
        glorified in him.
If God is glorified in him,
    God will also glorify him in himself,
    and God will glorify him at once.
My children, I will be with you only a little
    while longer.

I give you a new commandment: love one another.
As I have loved you, so you also should love
    one another.
This is how all will know that you are my disciples,
    if you have love for one another."

The Gospel of the Lord.

EXPLANATION OF THE READING

Jesus' command to "love one another" is so simple that a child can
understand it. It seems to make perfect sense. Jesus loves us; and we are
to love others with that same love. In so doing, the world will recognize us
as followers of Christ. It is so simple to say, yet so difficult to do. We do
love each other, but nevertheless we strive with one another. We listen
to each other, but too often we are so intent upon our own way of doing
things that we fail to hear what others are saying. But those three little
words keep calling us back to the simple challenge of the Gospel message:
"Love one another."

May 9, 2010

SIXTH SUNDAY OF EASTER

A reading from the holy Gospel according to John

14:23–29

Jesus said to his disciples:
    "Whoever loves me will keep my word,
    and my Father will love him,
    and we will come to him and make our dwelling
        with him.

Whoever does not love me does not keep my words;
  yet the word you hear is not mine
  but that of the Father who sent me.

"I have told you this while I am with you.
The Advocate, the Holy Spirit,
  whom the Father will send in my name,
  will teach you everything
  and remind you of all that I told you.
Peace I leave with you; my peace I give to you.
Not as the world gives do I give it to you.
Do not let your hearts be troubled or afraid.
You heard me tell you,
  'I am going away and I will come back to you.'
If you loved me,
  you would rejoice that I am going to the Father;
  for the Father is greater than I.
And now I have told you this before it happens,
  so that when it happens you may believe."

The Gospel of the Lord.

EXPLANATION OF THE READING

As the Easter season draws to a close, our readings begin to anticipate the Ascension of the Lord and the coming of the Holy Spirit at Pentecost. Jesus tells his disciples what the role of the Holy Spirit will be. He will be the "Advocate"—speaking on their behalf. He will be a teacher; in fact, he will teach them "everything" and remind them of all Jesus said. We need not be afraid, for through the Holy Spirit Jesus keeps his promise to remain with us always.

May 13 or May 16, 2010

SOLEMNITY OF THE ASCENSION OF THE LORD

A reading from the holy Gospel according to Luke

24:46–53

Jesus said to his disciples:
"Thus it is written that the Christ would suffer
and rise from the dead on the third day
and that repentance, for the forgiveness of sins,
would be preached in his name
to all the nations, beginning from Jerusalem.
You are witnesses of these things.
And behold I am sending the promise of my Father
upon you;
but stay in the city
until you are clothed with power from on high."

Then he led them out as far as Bethany,
raised his hands, and blessed them.
As he blessed them he parted from them
and was taken up to heaven.
They did him homage
and then returned to Jerusalem with great joy,
and they were continually in the temple
praising God.

The Gospel of the Lord.

EXPLANATION OF THE READING

The Ascension completes what the Incarnation began. Christ came down from heaven, and now he returns to his Father. In these, Christ's last moments on earth, Christ continues doing what he has done from the start: he teaches and blesses. Even as he ascends to the right hand of the Father, his thoughts are with his disciples, and he blesses them as he goes. The place of the Ascension is significant: he does not leave them from the mount of Transfiguration, nor from the hill of Calvary. Instead, he parts from them in Bethany, where he had raised Lazarus from the dead, and where he had spent so many hours in the company of his friends.

May 16, 2010

SEVENTH SUNDAY OF EASTER

A reading from the holy Gospel according to John
17:20–26

Lifting up his eyes to heaven, Jesus prayed, saying:
  "Holy Father, I pray not only for them,
  but also for those who will believe in me through
    their word,
  so that they may all be one,
  as you, Father, are in me and I in you,
  that they also may be in us,
  that the world may believe that you sent me.
And I have given them the glory you gave me,
  so that they may be one, as we are one,
  I in them and you in me,
  that they may be brought to perfection as one,
  that the world may know that you sent me,
  and that you loved them even as you loved me.
Father, they are your gift to me.

I wish that where I am they also may be with me,
  that they may see my glory that you gave me,
  because you loved me before the foundation
    of the world.
Righteous Father, the world also does not know you,
  but I know you, and they know that you sent me.
I made known to them your name and I will make
    it known,
  that the love with which you loved me
  may be in them and I in them."

The Gospel of the Lord.

EXPLANATION OF THE READING

Christ prays to his Father. It is for us that he prays. His prayer expresses his dream for us: a dream that only Christ—who is hope itself, love itself—could envision. He prays that his followers may be so perfect, so united, that the world may recognize the presence and the love of God. We are still far from being able to offer this perfect witness to God's love. Do we continue to hope for it? Work for it? Do we look forward to the perfect unity that will be ours in Christ's kingdom?

May 23, 2010

SOLEMNITY OF PENTECOST

A reading from the holy Gospel according to John
14:15–16, 23b–26

Jesus said to his disciples:
  "If you love me, you will keep my commandments.

And I will ask the Father,
. and he will give you another Advocate to be
    with you always.

"Whoever loves me will keep my word,
    and my Father will love him,
    and we will come to him and make our dwelling
        with him.
Those who do not love me do not keep my words;
    yet the word you hear is not mine
    but that of the Father who sent me.

"I have told you this while I am with you.
The Advocate, the Holy Spirit whom the Father will
        send in my name,
    will teach you everything
    and remind you of all that I told you."

The Gospel of the Lord.

Alternative form: John 20:19–23

EXPLANATION OF THE READING

As the risen Christ sends the apostles in mission, he bestows the gift of
the Holy Spirit upon them for the forgiveness of sin. He entrusts to them
not only his mission, but the fruit of that mission, redemption, and
forgiveness. The apostles, having received the blessing of the Lord's peace,
are to be its ministers. As a communion of reconciled sinners, the Church
shares the gift she has first received.

Ordinary Time during Summer and Fall

May 30, 2010

Solemnity of the Most Holy Trinity

A reading from the holy Gospel according to John

16:12–15

Jesus said to his disciples:
  "I have much more to tell you, but you cannot
    bear it now.
But when he comes, the Spirit of truth,
  he will guide you to all truth.
He will not speak on his own,
  but he will speak what he hears,
  and will declare to you the things that are coming.
He will glorify me,
  because he will take from what is mine and declare
    it to you.
Everything that the Father has is mine;
  for this reason I told you that he will take from
    what is mine
  and declare it to you."

The Gospel of the Lord.

Jesus tells his disciples that the promised gift of the Holy Spirit will guide them into all truth and glorify Jesus. The truth is not a series of verifiable propositions or claims about reality, but a relationship with the one who is God's truth. We are invited to share in a relationship with the one who exists in the communion of love that is Father, Son, and Holy Spirit.

June 6, 2010

SOLEMNITY OF THE MOST HOLY BODY AND BLOOD OF CHRIST

A reading from the holy Gospel according to Luke

9:11b–17

Jesus spoke to the crowds about the kingdom of God,
  and he healed those who needed to be cured.
As the day was drawing to a close,
  the Twelve approached him and said,
  "Dismiss the crowd
  so that they can go to the surrounding villages
    and farms
  and find lodging and provisions;
  for we are in a deserted place here."
He said to them, "Give them some food yourselves."
They replied, "Five loaves and two fish are all we have,
  unless we ourselves go and buy food for all
    these people."
Now the men there numbered about five thousand.
Then he said to his disciples,
  "Have them sit down in groups of about fifty."

They did so and made them all sit down.
Then taking the five loaves and the two fish,
    and looking up to heaven,
    he said the blessing over them, broke them,
    and gave them to the disciples to set before
        the crowd.
They all ate and were satisfied.
And when the leftover fragments were picked up,
    they filled twelve wicker baskets.

The Gospel of the Lord.

EXPLANATION OF THE READING

The multiplication of the loaves is one of the only miracles that is recounted in all four Gospels accounts. In giving us this story on this solemnity of the Body and Blood of Christ, the Church urges us to see in it an emblem of the Eucharist. Notice how Jesus divides the great assembly into smaller units, "groups of about fifty"—no longer crowds, but communities. Then he looks up to heaven and gives thanks, and in turn commissions the disciples to carry the bread and fish to the people. In Eucharist, it is Christ who works the wonder, but he uses human instruments: priests and people. And "all ate and were satisfied." When Jesus comes to us in the Eucharist, faith tells us that it is not a piece or portion that we receive— but the whole Christ, a feast for body and soul.

June 13, 2010

ELEVENTH SUNDAY IN ORDINARY TIME

A reading from the holy Gospel according to Luke

7:36–50

A Pharisee invited Jesus to dine with him,
    and he entered the Pharisee's house and
        reclined at table.
Now there was a sinful woman in the city
    who learned that he was at table in the house of
        the Pharisee.
Bringing an alabaster flask of ointment,
    she stood behind him at his feet weeping
    and began to bathe his feet with her tears.
Then she wiped them with her hair,
    kissed them, and anointed them with the ointment.
When the Pharisee who had invited him saw this
        he said to himself,
    "If this man were a prophet,
    he would know who and what sort of woman this
        is who is touching him,
    that she is a sinner."
Jesus said to him in reply,
    "Simon, I have something to say to you."
"Tell me, teacher," he said.
"Two people were in debt to a certain creditor;
    one owed five hundred day's wages and the other
        owed fifty.

Since they were unable to repay the debt, he forgave
 it for both.
Which of them will love him more?"
Simon said in reply,
 "The one, I suppose, whose larger debt
 was forgiven."
He said to him, "You have judged rightly."
Then he turned to the woman and said to Simon,
 "Do you see this woman?
When I entered your house, you did not give me water
 for my feet,
 but she has bathed them with her tears
 and wiped them with her hair.
You did not give me a kiss,
 but she has not ceased kissing my feet since
 the time I entered.
You did not anoint my head with oil,
 but she anointed my feet with ointment.
So I tell you, her many sins have been forgiven
 because she has shown great love.
But the one to whom little is forgiven, loves little."
He said to her, "Your sins are forgiven."
The others at table said to themselves,
 "Who is this who even forgives sins?"
But he said to the woman,
 "Your faith has saved you; go in peace."

The Gospel of the Lord.

Longer form: Luke 7:36—8:3

EXPLANATION OF THE READING

Forgiveness is mentioned so many times in the Gospel. It is the subject of many of Jesus' parables. Why is forgiveness so important? This wonderful story gives us a clue. The sinful woman who comes to Simon's house shows incredible, tender love and care for Jesus. She gets down on her hands and knees and anoints his feet, weeping with emotion. She dries his feet with her own hair (think of what Saint Paul said: that a woman's hair is "her glory" [1 Corinthians 11:15]). And Jesus tells us how she is able to love in this way: because "her many sins have been forgiven." Forgiveness leads to love. That is why we must forgive.

June 20, 2010

TWELFTH SUNDAY IN ORDINARY TIME

A reading from the holy Gospel according to Luke

Luke 9:18–24

Once when Jesus was praying in solitude,
 and the disciples were with him,
  he asked them, "Who do the crowds say that I am?"
They said in reply, "John the Baptist;
 others, Elijah;
 still others, 'One of the ancient prophets
  has arisen.'"
Then he said to them, "But who do you say that I am?"
Peter said in reply, "The Christ of God."
He rebuked them
 and directed them not to tell this to anyone.

He said, "The Son of Man must suffer greatly
  and be rejected by the elders, the chief priests,
    and the scribes,
  and be killed and on the third day be raised."

Then he said to all,
  "If anyone wishes to come after me, he must
    deny himself
  and take up his cross daily and follow me.
For whoever wishes to save his life will lose it,
  but whoever loses his life for my sake will save it."

The Gospel of the Lord.

EXPLANATION OF THE READING

The Christian life is full of paradox. It is a life of joy—that was the
hallmark of the early Christians—but as Jesus forcefully reminds the
disciples, it is a life of suffering as well. To be a Christian is to carry the
cross—but to rejoice as we do so, knowing that Jesus carries it with us
and for us.

June 27, 2010

THIRTEENTH SUNDAY IN ORDINARY TIME

A reading from the holy Gospel according to Luke
9:51–62

When the days for Jesus' being taken up were fulfilled,
  he resolutely determined to journey to Jerusalem,
  and he sent messengers ahead of him.

On the way they entered a Samaritan village
    to prepare for his reception there,
    but they would not welcome him
    because the destination of his journey was
        Jerusalem.
When the disciples James and John saw this
        they asked,
    "Lord, do you want us to call down fire from heaven
    to consume them?"
Jesus turned and rebuked them, and they journeyed
        to another village.

As they were proceeding on their journey someone
        said to him,
    "I will follow you wherever you go."
Jesus answered him,
    "Foxes have dens and birds of the sky have nests,
    but the Son of Man has nowhere to rest his head."
And to another he said, "Follow me."
But he replied, "Lord, let me go first and bury
        my father."
But he answered him, "Let the dead bury their dead.
But you, go and proclaim the kingdom of God."

And another said, "I will follow you, Lord,
    but first let me say farewell to my family at home."
To him Jesus said, "No one who sets a hand to
        the plow

and looks to what was left behind is fit for
   the kingdom of God."

The Gospel of the Lord.

EXPLANATION OF THE READING

In this reading we can almost taste the dust of the hard roads Jesus walked
on his way to Jerusalem. It is a challenging Gospel, for the three people
who approach Jesus in turn are so human, and Jesus' responses to them
are so divine. To the one who exclaims in his enthusiasm, "I will follow
you wherever you go," Jesus says that to follow the Son of Man means to
be homeless, uprooted. To those who hesitate, wanting to settle accounts,
say good-bye, Jesus says, do not look back. It seems that the new life of
discipleship is not something we can ease ourselves into. We must plunge
in headlong, leaving the dead past behind, trusting that if we follow in the
footsteps of Christ, God will provide.

July 4, 2010

FOURTEENTH SUNDAY IN ORDINARY TIME

A reading from the holy Gospel according to Luke

10:1–9

At that time the Lord appointed seventy-two others
   whom he sent ahead of him in pairs
   to every town and place he intended to visit.
He said to them,
   "The harvest is abundant but the laborers are few;
   so ask the master of the harvest
   to send out laborers for his harvest.
Go on your way;
   behold, I am sending you like lambs among wolves.

Carry no money bag, no sack, no sandals;
   and greet no one along the way.
Into whatever house you enter, first say,
   'Peace to this household.'
If a peaceful person lives there,
   your peace will rest on him;
   but if not, it will return to you.
Stay in the same house and eat and drink what
      is offered to you,
   for the laborer deserves his payment.
Do not move about from one house to another.
Whatever town you enter and they welcome you,
   eat what is set before you,
   cure the sick in it and say to them,
   'The kingdom of God is at hand for you.'"

The Gospel of the Lord.

Longer form: Luke 10:1–12, 17–20

EXPLANATION OF THE READING

Jesus sends out the 72 disciples with very specific "rules for the road," many of them having to do with the hospitality the disciples are to seek and accept from others. Once they enter a house, they are to stay there, not moving about from place to place. They are to eat whatever is set before them. In short, they are to share the lives of those to whom they preach the Gospel. But these empty-handed itinerant preachers have a gift to give also. They enter with a blessing of peace, and they bring with them Christ's own healing—and the Good News of the kingdom of God.

July 11, 2010

FIFTEENTH SUNDAY
IN ORDINARY TIME

A reading from the holy Gospel according to Luke

10:25–37

There was a scholar of the law who stood up to test
    Jesus and said,
  "Teacher, what must I do to inherit eternal life?"
Jesus said to him, "What is written in the law?
How do you read it?"
He said in reply,
  "You shall love the Lord, your God,
  with all your heart,
  with all your being,
  with all your strength,
  and with all your mind,
  and your neighbor as yourself."
He replied to him, "You have answered correctly;
  do this and you will live."

But because he wished to justify himself,
    he said to Jesus,
  "And who is my neighbor?"
Jesus replied,
  "A man fell victim to robbers
  as he went down from Jerusalem to Jericho.
They stripped and beat him and went off leaving
    him half-dead.

A priest happened to be going down that road,
   but when he saw him, he passed by on
      the opposite side.
Likewise a Levite came to the place,
   and when he saw him, he passed by on
      the opposite side.
But a Samaritan traveler who came upon him
   was moved with compassion at the sight.
He approached the victim,
   poured oil and wine over his wounds and
      bandaged them.
Then he lifted him up on his own animal,
   took him to an inn, and cared for him.
The next day he took out two silver coins
   and gave them to the innkeeper with the instruction,
      'Take care of him.
If you spend more than what I have given you,
   I shall repay you on my way back.'
Which of these three, in your opinion,
   was neighbor to the robbers' victim?"
He answered, "The one who treated him with mercy."
Jesus said to him, "Go and do likewise."

The Gospel of the Lord.

EXPLANATION OF THE READING

To be a Christian is to be a neighbor. To be a neighbor is to show mercy.
The parable of the good Samaritan reveals that we are neighbors not
by nearness or by race or by profession. We only become neighbors when
we act with compassion. This Gospel is a call to examine our consciences.
Are we neighbors, in this Gospel sense of the word, to those who are
closest to us? Do we act with love and compassion? And what about when

we are hurting—do we accept love from those we consider outsiders—
from the Samaritans in our communities?

July 18, 2010

SIXTEENTH SUNDAY IN ORDINARY TIME

A reading from the holy Gospel according to Luke

10:38–42

Jesus entered a village
  where a woman whose name was Martha
    welcomed him.
She had a sister named Mary
  who sat beside the Lord at his feet listening
    to him speak.
Martha, burdened with much serving, came to him
    and said,
  "Lord, do you not care
  that my sister has left me by myself to do
    the serving?
Tell her to help me."
The Lord said to her in reply,
  "Martha, Martha, you are anxious and worried
    about many things.
There is need of only one thing.
Mary has chosen the better part
  and it will not be taken from her."

The Gospel of the Lord.

EXPLANATION OF THE READING

The tension in this familiar Gospel is one that exists within every community—perhaps within each person. Mary and Martha both eagerly welcome Jesus to their home. But while Martha bustles around getting things ready—no doubt preparing a special meal for this honored guest— Mary simply sits at his feet and listens. And—to Martha's surprise—Jesus tells her that Mary has made the better choice. Perhaps the long days of summer are a good time to step away from our constant busy-ness and to do a little quiet reflecting at the Lord's feet. May we find with Mary the treasure that cannot be taken away.

July 25, 2010

SEVENTEENTH SUNDAY IN ORDINARY TIME

A reading from the holy Gospel according to Luke   11:1–13

Jesus was praying in a certain place,
    and when he had finished,
    one of his disciples said to him,
    "Lord, teach us to pray just as John taught
        his disciples."
He said to them, "When you pray, say:
    Father, hallowed be your name,
        your kingdom come.
        Give us each day our daily bread
        and forgive us our sins
        for we ourselves forgive everyone in debt to us,
        and do not subject us to the final test."

And he said to them, "Suppose one of you has a friend
   to whom he goes at midnight and says,
   'Friend, lend me three loaves of bread,
   for a friend of mine has arrived at my house
      from a journey
   and I have nothing to offer him,'
   and he says in reply from within,
   'Do not bother me; the door has already been locked
   and my children and I are already in bed.
I cannot get up to give you anything.'
I tell you,
   if he does not get up to give the visitor the loaves
   because of their friendship,
   he will get up to give him whatever he needs
   because of his persistence.

"And I tell you, ask and you will receive;
   seek and you will find;
   knock and the door will be opened to you.
For everyone who asks, receives;
   and the one who seeks, finds;
   and to the one who knocks, the door will be opened.
What father among you would hand his son a snake
   when he asks for a fish?
Or hand him a scorpion when he asks for an egg?
If you then, who are wicked,
   know how to give good gifts to your children,

how much more will the Father in heaven
give the Holy Spirit to those who ask him?"

The Gospel of the Lord.

EXPLANATION OF THE READING

Imagine watching Jesus at prayer. In today's Gospel the disciples watch
Jesus pray, and when he is finished, they ask him to teach them how to
pray. Jesus gives them a prayer—simple words of praise and petition,
forgiveness, and reconciliation. He also gives them an attitude for prayer.
Though the words are simple, they must be disciplined. Persistence—
unceasing and untiring persistence—must be the attitude of all who offer
prayer to God. God will hear us: but we must ask, seek, and knock
unceasingly.

August 1, 2010

EIGHTEENTH SUNDAY
IN ORDINARY TIME

A reading from the holy Gospel
according to Luke   *12:13–21*

Someone in the crowd said to Jesus,
   "Teacher, tell my brother to share the inheritance
      with me."
He replied to him,
   "Friend, who appointed me as your judge and
      arbitrator?"
Then he said to the crowd,
   "Take care to guard against all greed,
   for though one may be rich,
   one's life does not consist of possessions."

Then he told them a parable.

"There was a rich man whose land produced
    a bountiful harvest.
He asked himself, 'What shall I do,
    for I do not have space to store my harvest?'
And he said, 'This is what I shall do:
    I shall tear down my barns and build larger ones.
There I shall store all my grain and other goods
    and I shall say to myself, "Now as for you,
    you have so many good things stored up
        for many years,
    rest, eat, drink, be merry!"'
But God said to him,
    'You fool, this night your life will be demanded
        of you;
    and the things you have prepared,
        to whom will they belong?'
Thus will it be for all who store up treasure
    for themselves
    but are not rich in what matters to God."

The Gospel of the Lord.

EXPLANATION OF THE READING

Jesus' teaching is not only counter-cultural; sometimes it runs counter to
our human nature. The person in the crowd who asks Jesus to mediate
between him and his brother is only asking for what is his own—he only
wants what is fair. Jesus' reply must have seemed very harsh—"guard
against all greed." For us, too, that response is hard to hear. How often
does self-interest motivate even our good actions? Jesus tells a parable to
remind his listeners that no matter how much wealth we accumulate, our
lives are still in the hands of God. We must not allow money and material

things—even those that rightfully belong to us—to come between us and our neighbor—between us and God.

August 8, 2010

Nineteenth Sunday in Ordinary Time

A reading from the holy Gospel according to Luke $\qquad$ 12:35–40

Jesus said to his disciples:
  "Gird your loins and light your lamps
  and be like servants who await their master's
    return from a wedding,
  ready to open immediately when he comes
    and knocks.
Blessed are those servants
  whom the master finds vigilant on his arrival.
Amen, I say to you, he will gird himself,
  have them recline at table, and proceed to wait
    on them.
And should he come in the second or third watch
  and find them prepared in this way,
  blessed are those servants.
Be sure of this:
  if the master of the house had known the hour
  when the thief was coming,
  he would not have let his house be broken into.

You also must be prepared, for at an hour you
   do not expect,
   the Son of Man will come."

The Gospel of the Lord.

Longer form: Luke 12:32–48

EXPLANATION OF THE READING

The parable likens God to a master who has gone away on a journey. His
servants who remain at home must be "vigilant," staying awake at all times
because they are not sure when he will arrive. But this is a different kind
of master. When he comes home, instead of expecting to be waited on,
he himself takes on the garb of a slave, and waits on his faithful servants.
The Master we serve loves us so much that he stoops to wash our feet.
And we must reciprocate by serving others, by living the Gospel life.

August 15, 2010

SOLEMNITY OF THE ASSUMPTION OF THE BLESSED VIRGIN MARY

A reading from the holy Gospel according to Luke

1:39–56

Mary set out
   and traveled to the hill country in haste
   to a town of Judah,
   where she entered the house of Zechariah
   and greeted Elizabeth.
When Elizabeth heard Mary's greeting,
   the infant leaped in her womb,
   and Elizabeth, filled with the Holy Spirit,

cried out in a loud voice and said,
"Blessed are you among women,
and blessed is the fruit of your womb.
And how does this happen to me,
that the mother of my Lord should come to me?
For at the moment the sound of your greeting
reached my ears,
the infant in my womb leaped for joy.
Blessed are you who believed
that what was spoken to you by the Lord
would be fulfilled."

And Mary said:

"My soul proclaims the greatness of the Lord;
my spirit rejoices in God my Savior
for he has looked with favor on his lowly servant.
From this day all generations will call me blessed:
the Almighty has done great things for me
and holy is his Name.
He has mercy on those who fear him
in every generation.
He has shown the strength of his arm,
and has scattered the proud in their conceit.
He has cast down the mighty from their thrones,
and has lifted up the lowly.
He has filled the hungry with good things,
and the rich he has sent away empty.

He has come to the help of his servant Israel
 for he has remembered his promise of mercy,
 the promise he made to our fathers,
 to Abraham and his children for ever."

Mary remained with her about three months
 and then returned to her home.

The Gospel of the Lord.

EXPLANATION OF THE READING

On this day when Mary was taken into heaven, the Gospel seems to bring
us down to earth. A crowd listens eagerly to the teaching of Jesus, and one
woman cannot contain her praise. She calls out to him, blessing his
mother. But Jesus corrects her. It was not in carrying the Word-made-flesh
in her womb, in nursing him at her breast, that Mary became blessed.
Rather, it is because of her total obedience to God's word, her life of faith,
that Mary is "blessed among women." All who hear the word of God are
also called to holiness. Mary's call to holiness, then, is our call; and this
feast of Mary's is ours as well. We believe that Mary was taken body and
soul into heaven. And we believe that we will one day share in that glory.
As we profess in the Creed: "We look to the resurrection of the dead, and
the life of the world to come." This is a day for rejoicing. It is Mary's feast
day; but it is also our own.

August 22, 2010

Twenty-first Sunday in Ordinary Time

A reading from the holy Gospel according to Luke

13:22–30

Jesus passed through towns and villages,
  teaching as he went and making his way
    to Jerusalem.
Someone asked him,
  "Lord, will only a few people be saved?"
He answered them,
  "Strive to enter through the narrow gate,
  for many, I tell you, will attempt to enter
  but will not be strong enough.
After the master of the house has arisen and locked
    the door,
  then will you stand outside knocking and saying,
  'Lord, open the door for us.'
He will say to you in reply,
  'I do not know where you are from.'
And you will say,
  'We ate and drank in your company and you taught
    in our streets.'
Then he will say to you,
  'I do not know where you are from.
Depart from me, all you evildoers!'
And there will be wailing and grinding of teeth
  when you see Abraham, Isaac, and Jacob

and all the prophets in the kingdom of God
and you yourselves cast out.
And people will come from the east and the west
and from the north and the south
and will recline at table in the kingdom of God.
For behold, some are last who will be first,
and some are first who will be last."

The Gospel of the Lord.

EXPLANATION OF THE READING

This is a beautiful vision of the kingdom of God: people from every corner of the earth, "from the east and the west and from the north and the south," recline at table together with the Lord in a never-ending banquet. But not all are inside; among those who remain outside knocking are people who claim acquaintance with the Master: "We ate and drank in your company and you taught in our streets!" But twice the host repeats the words, "I do not know where you are from." We, too, eat and drink with the Lord, and we hear his word, every time we celebrate the Eucharist. That in itself is not enough. Do we really get to know the Lord through prayer? Do we meet him in the poor, the afflicted, the abandoned?

August 29, 2010

TWENTY-SECOND SUNDAY IN ORDINARY TIME

A reading from the holy Gospel according to Luke
14:1, 7–14

On a sabbath Jesus went to dine
at the home of one of the leading Pharisees,
and the people there were observing him carefully.

He told a parable to those who had been invited,
noticing how they were choosing the places
of honor at the table.
"When you are invited by someone to
a wedding banquet,
do not recline at table in the place of honor.
A more distinguished guest than you may have been
invited by him,
and the host who invited both of you may approach
you and say,
'Give your place to this man,'
and then you would proceed with embarrassment
to take the lowest place.
Rather, when you are invited,
go and take the lowest place
so that when the host comes to you he may say,
'My friend, move up to a higher position.'
Then you will enjoy the esteem of your companions
at the table.
For everyone who exalts himself will be humbled,
but the one who humbles himself will be exalted."
Then he said to the host who invited him,
"When you hold a lunch or a dinner,
do not invite your friends or your brothers
or your relatives or your wealthy neighbors,
in case they may invite you back and
you have repayment.
Rather, when you hold a banquet,
invite the poor, the crippled, the lame, the blind;

blessed indeed will you be because of their inability
to repay you.
For you will be repaid at the resurrection
of the righteous."

The Gospel of the Lord.

EXPLANATION OF THE READING

The Pharisees scrutinize every action of Jesus, always looking for some
way to catch him. Jesus is watching them as well—and as he eats supper
at the house of one of their leaders, he notices how all the people seek the
places of honor at the table. In a parable, Jesus teaches that instead of
seeking the highest place, they should seek the lowest place; that way, the
host, instead of sending them down the table when someone important
comes in, will ask them to move up to a better place. What Jesus is
speaking of, of course, is not a banquet like the one at which they are
sitting, but the kingdom of God. Instead of congratulating ourselves on
our righteousness—like the law-abiding Pharisees—we must seek "the
lowest place," coming to God on our knees, and letting God be the one to
raise us up.

September 5, 2010

TWENTY-THIRD SUNDAY
IN ORDINARY TIME

A reading from the holy Gospel
according to Luke
14:25–33

Great crowds were traveling with Jesus,
and he turned and addressed them,
"If anyone comes to me without hating his father
and mother,
wife and children, brothers and sisters,

and even his own life,
   he cannot be my disciple.
Whoever does not carry his own cross and
      come after me
   cannot be my disciple.
Which of you wishing to construct a tower
   does not first sit down and calculate the cost
   to see if there is enough for its completion?
Otherwise, after laying the foundation
   and finding himself unable to finish the work
   the onlookers should laugh at him and say,
   'This one began to build but did not have
      the resources to finish.'
Or what king marching into battle would not first
      sit down
   and decide whether with ten thousand troops
   he can successfully oppose another king
   advancing upon him with twenty thousand troops?
But if not, while he is still far away,
   he will send a delegation to ask for peace terms.
In the same way,
   anyone of you who does not renounce all
      his possessions
   cannot be my disciple."

The Gospel of the Lord.

EXPLANATION OF THE READING

To those who are journeying with him, Jesus addresses a series of parables, all of which ask one basic question: Do we know the cost of discipleship? Can we afford it? Living the Gospel will not be a small project, one that can be finished in a day or two—or even a year or two. Following Jesus is an enormous undertaking, like building a tower, or leading a great army into battle. Before we begin, we must be sure that we can "afford" it. Following Jesus will cost us—it will take everything we have.

September 12, 2010

Twenty-fourth Sunday in Ordinary Time

A reading from the holy Gospel according to Luke

15:1–10

Tax collectors and sinners were all drawing near
    to listen to Jesus,
  but the Pharisees and scribes began to complain,
    saying,
  "This man welcomes sinners and eats with them."
So to them he addressed this parable.
"What man among you having a hundred sheep and
    losing one of them
  would not leave the ninety-nine in the desert
  and go after the lost one until he finds it?
And when he does find it,
  he sets it on his shoulders with great joy
  and, upon his arrival home,
  he calls together his friends and neighbors and
    says to them,
  'Rejoice with me because I have found
    my lost sheep.'

I tell you, in just the same way
   there will be more joy in heaven over one sinner
      who repents
   than over ninety-nine righteous people
   who have no need of repentance.

"Or what woman having ten coins and losing one
   would not light a lamp and sweep the house,
   searching carefully until she finds it?
And when she does find it,
   she calls together her friends and neighbors
   and says to them,
   'Rejoice with me because I have found the coin
      that I lost.'
In just the same way, I tell you,
   there will be rejoicing among the angels of God
   over one sinner who repents."

The Gospel of the Lord.

Longer form: Luke 15:1–32

EXPLANATION OF THE READING

Today's parable encapsulates the essence of Jesus' teaching about the Father. Our God is one who actively seeks us. We do not have to be pristine, totally without sin, in order to approach him; in fact, he actively searches out the grimiest souls in order to cleanse them and bring them to himself. So often we are lost in a world of consumerism, apathy, and self-absorption. Today, Jesus tells us that our God is calling to us; let's go home with him.

September 19, 2010

Twenty-fifth Sunday in Ordinary Time

A reading from the holy Gospel according to Luke

16:10–13

Jesus said to his disciples:
  "The person who is trustworthy in
      very small matters
  is also trustworthy in great ones;
  and the person who is dishonest in
      very small matters
  is also dishonest in great ones.
If, therefore, you are not trustworthy with
      dishonest wealth,
  who will trust you with true wealth?
If you are not trustworthy with what belongs
      to another,
  who will give you what is yours?
No servant can serve two masters.
He will either hate one and love the other,
  or be devoted to one and despise the other.
You cannot serve both God and mammon."

The Gospel of the Lord.

Longer form: Luke 16:1–13

Explanation of the Reading

Jesus often speaks about money. Letting go of it is one of the prerequisites of discipleship. He sends his disciples out without it—they are to carry no purse or moneybag. Why? Because Jesus knows how much money means to us. It is a means to an end that all too easily becomes an end in itself. Money means support for ourselves and our families, yes; but it also can come to mean status, security, even sense of self. We take care of it, invest it, watch it grow. Jesus knows we need money—that is, we need the things that money buys for us. But Jesus urges us to dedicate the energy and trust we give to money to God instead.

September 26, 2010

TWENTY-SIXTH SUNDAY IN ORDINARY TIME

A reading from the holy Gospel according to Luke

16:19–31

Jesus said to the Pharisees:
    "There was a rich man who dressed in
        purple garments and fine linen
    and dined sumptuously each day.
And lying at his door was a poor man named Lazarus,
        covered with sores,
    who would gladly have eaten his fill of the scraps
    that fell from the rich man's table.
Dogs even used to come and lick his sores.
When the poor man died,
    he was carried away by angels to the bosom
        of Abraham.
The rich man also died and was buried,
    and from the netherworld, where he was in torment,
    he raised his eyes and saw Abraham far off
    and Lazarus at his side.

And he cried out, 'Father Abraham, have pity on me.
Send Lazarus to dip the tip of his finger in water and
   cool my tongue,
   for I am suffering torment in these flames.'
Abraham replied,
   'My child, remember that you received
   what was good during your lifetime
   while Lazarus likewise received what was bad;
   but now he is comforted here, whereas you
   are tormented.
Moreover, between us and you a great chasm
   is established
   to prevent anyone from crossing who might wish
   to go
   from our side to yours or from your side to ours.'
He said, 'Then I beg you, father,
   send him to my father's house, for I have
   five brothers,
   so that he may warn them,
   lest they too come to this place of torment.'
But Abraham replied, 'They have Moses and
   the prophets.
Let them listen to them.'
He said, 'Oh no, father Abraham,
   but if someone from the dead goes to them,
   they will repent.'
Then Abraham said, 'If they will not listen to Moses
   and the prophets,

neither will they be persuaded if someone should
rise from the dead.'"

The Gospel of the Lord.

EXPLANATION OF THE READING

Lazarus never says a word in this parable. He is silent, as the poor and
the afflicted of our world so often are — not because they cannot speak,
but because they are not heard. Though silent, Lazarus is not invisible.
The rich man must have seen him every day, as he came and went from
his sumptuous dwelling. When the two men die, everything is turned
upside down. Lazarus is caught up by angels, and carried like something
most precious to the very arms of Abraham. The rich man, on the other
hand, goes down, to be tormented in flames. Abraham speaks to the
rich man pityingly, calling him "my child"; but it is too late. His brothers
have Moses and the prophets to warn them. They have other prophets
as well: the living Lazaruses on their doorsteps.

October 3, 2010

TWENTY-SEVENTH SUNDAY
IN ORDINARY TIME

A reading from the holy Gospel
according to Luke   *17:5–10*

The apostles said to the Lord, "Increase our faith."
The Lord replied,
  "If you have faith the size of a mustard seed,
  you would say to this mulberry tree,
  'Be uprooted and planted in the sea,'
      and it would obey you.

"Who among you would say to your servant
   who has just come in from plowing or
      tending sheep in the field,
   'Come here immediately and take your place
      at table'?
Would he not rather say to him,
   'Prepare something for me to eat.
Put on your apron and wait on me while I eat
   and drink.
You may eat and drink when I am finished'?
Is he grateful to that servant because he did what
      was commanded?
So should it be with you.
When you have done all you have been commanded,
   say, 'We are unprofitable servants;
      we have done what we were obliged to do.'"

The Gospel of the Lord.

EXPLANATION OF THE READING

Jesus reminds the apostles that they are not God's princes, or viceroys,
or politicians; rather, they are simply God's servants. They are to work
not for praise or reward, or even for rest after labor, but simply because
it is their duty to the Master they serve. How often do we do what we
do with the expectation of being noticed and rewarded? How often do
we become frustrated because we feel unrecognized, underpaid, or
unappreciated? No one ever rewarded servants more richly than Jesus,
who feeds us with his body and blood, stoops to wash our feet, and leads
us to share in his divine life. In this Gospel reading, Jesus reminds us of
the kind of attitude we should have in our work on behalf of the kingdom.
Our focus needs to be not on ourselves, but on God.

October 10, 2010

Twenty-eighth Sunday in Ordinary Time

A reading from the holy Gospel according to Luke

17:11–19

As Jesus continued his journey to Jerusalem,
  he traveled through Samaria and Galilee.
As he was entering a village, ten lepers met him.
They stood at a distance from him and raised
    their voices, saying,
  "Jesus, Master! Have pity on us!"
And when he saw them, he said,
  "Go show yourselves to the priests."
As they were going they were cleansed.
And one of them, realizing he had been healed,
  returned, glorifying God in a loud voice;
  and he fell at the feet of Jesus and thanked him.
He was a Samaritan.
Jesus said in reply,
  "Ten were cleansed, were they not?
Where are the other nine?
Has none but this foreigner returned to give thanks
    to God?"
Then he said to him, "Stand up and go;
  your faith has saved you."

The Gospel of the Lord.

EXPLANATION OF THE READING

The ten lepers seem very much alike. They approach Jesus in a body, and they cry out to him with one voice, "Have pity on us!" And Jesus cures them all at the same time, with a word. But the lepers are not all alike. When they realize they are cured of their leprosy, nine of them dutifully plod on to show themselves to the priest. But one, in joy and amazement, turns back, "glorifying God in a loud voice," falling at the feet of Jesus to thank him. Jesus marvels that only one of the ten should come back to give thanks, and he sees this simple act of thanksgiving as a sign of great faith. It is not enough just to experience God's blessings in our lives; we must also recognize those blessings and give thanks. Our evening examination of conscience is a good time to do this. Looking back over the day, we can more easily recognize God's mercies—and say "thank you" at the feet of the Lord.

October 17, 2010

TWENTY-NINTH SUNDAY IN ORDINARY TIME

A reading from the holy Gospel according to Luke

18:1–8

Jesus told his disciples a parable
   about the necessity for them to pray always
      without becoming weary.
He said, "There was a judge in a certain town
   who neither feared God nor respected any
      human being.
And a widow in that town used to come to him
      and say,
   'Render a just decision for me against my adversary.'
For a long time the judge was unwilling,
      but eventually he thought,

'While it is true that I neither fear God nor respect
   any human being,
because this widow keeps bothering me
I shall deliver a just decision for her
lest she finally come and strike me.'"
The Lord said, "Pay attention to what
   the dishonest judge says.
Will not God then secure the rights of his chosen ones
   who call out to him day and night?
Will he be slow to answer them?
I tell you, he will see to it that justice is done
   for them speedily.
But when the Son of Man comes, will he find faith
   on earth?"

The Gospel of the Lord.

EXPLANATION OF THE READING

It is hard not to like both the characters in this Gospel parable—the
widow and the judge. The widow is steady, courageous, and persistent in
her quest for justice. The judge, while he is both unkind and unjust, is
refreshingly honest in his reflections on himself and his motivations. Jesus
uses this unjust judge to point to the mercy of God. If this flawed human
judge can render a just decision, how can we doubt that God, who is truth
and justice itself, will grant justice to those "who call out to him day and
night"? Will we be persistent, like the widow of the parable, praying in
hope even if the answer is long in coming?

October 24, 2010

Thirtieth Sunday in Ordinary Time

A reading from the holy Gospel according to Luke

18:9–14

Jesus addressed this parable
    to those who were convinced of their own
        righteousness
    and despised everyone else.
"Two people went up to the temple area to pray;
    one was a Pharisee and the other was
        a tax collector.
The Pharisee took up his position and spoke
    this prayer to himself,
    'O God, I thank you that I am not like the rest
        of humanity—
    greedy, dishonest, adulterous—or even like
        this tax collector.
I fast twice a week, and I pay tithes on
    my whole income.'
But the tax collector stood off at a distance
    and would not even raise his eyes to heaven
    but beat his breast and prayed,
    'O God, be merciful to me a sinner.'
I tell you, the latter went home justified,
    not the former;

for whoever exalts himself will be humbled,
and the one who humbles himself will be exalted."

The Gospel of the Lord.

EXPLANATION OF THE READING

Jesus reserves his harshest criticism not for sinners—to whom he is
unfailingly gentle—but for the self-righteous. In this parable, he gives God's
perspective on the prayers of two men, who both stand in the temple area,
praying. Notice the words of the Pharisee. First he rejects humanity in
general—they are all "greedy, dishonest, adulterous," he says—and then
he rejects humanity in particular, in the shape of the tax collector. The
Pharisee sees no good in others, no evil in himself. The tax collector, in
contrast, comes before God not lamenting the sins of others, but aware of
his own—he beats his breast and asks for mercy. The prayer God hears is
the prayer of the humble heart.

October 31, 2010

THIRTY-FIRST SUNDAY IN ORDINARY TIME

A reading from the holy Gospel according to Luke

19:1–10

At that time, Jesus came to Jericho and intended
    to pass through the town.
Now a man there named Zacchaeus,
  who was a chief tax collector and also
    a wealthy man,
  was seeking to see who Jesus was;
  but he could not see him because of the crowd,
  for he was short in stature.

So he ran ahead and climbed a sycamore tree
    in order to see Jesus,
  who was about to pass that way.
When he reached the place, Jesus looked up and said,
    "Zacchaeus, come down quickly,
  for today I must stay at your house."
And he came down quickly and received him with joy.
When they all saw this, they began to grumble, saying,
    "He has gone to stay at the house of a sinner."
But Zacchaeus stood there and said to the Lord,
    "Behold, half of my possessions, Lord,
      I shall give to the poor,
    and if I have extorted anything from anyone
    I shall repay it four times over."
And Jesus said to him,
    "Today salvation has come to this house
    because this man too is a descendant of Abraham.
For the Son of Man has come to seek
    and to save what was lost."

The Gospel of the Lord.

EXPLANATION OF THE READING

The story of Zaccheus is a wonderful metaphor for the spiritual life.
Zaccheus is not exactly a good man. He is a tax collector, and it seems he
has extorted money for himself on the side, thus becoming quite wealthy.
But sinner though he is, Zaccheus is curious about Jesus and climbs a tree
to get a look at him—perhaps also to stay at a safe distance from him. But
when Jesus looks at him, and calls him, Zaccheus responds "quickly" and
"with joy," and with full, voluntary repentance for the wrong he has done.
Then, Jesus comes to him at his table. It is the same for us. Drawn to
Jesus, we hardly know why, we glimpse him from afar. But then Jesus calls
us into a closer relationship with him. He forgives our sins, and he invites
us to feast at his table.

November 1, 2010

SOLEMNITY OF ALL SAINTS

A reading from the holy Gospel according to Matthew

5:1–12a

When Jesus saw the crowds, he went up
    the mountain,
and after he had sat down, his disciples came
    to him.
He began to teach them, saying:

"Blessed are the poor in spirit,
    for theirs is the Kingdom of heaven.
Blessed are they who mourn,
    for they will be comforted.
Blessed are the meek,
    for they will inherit the land.
Blessed are they who hunger and thirst
    for righteousness,
    for they will be satisfied.
Blessed are the merciful,
    for they will be shown mercy.
Blessed are the clean of heart,
    for they will see God.
Blessed are the peacemakers,
    for they will be called children of God.
Blessed are they who are persecuted for the sake
    of righteousness,
    for theirs is the Kingdom of heaven.

Blessed are you when they insult you and
    persecute you
and utter every kind of evil against you falsely
    because of me.
Rejoice and be glad,
    for your reward will be great in heaven."

The Gospel of the Lord.

EXPLANATION OF THE READING

On this day, the Church gives honor to all the saints—those whose names
we know, and those whose names are known only to God. We remember
all who lived the Beatitudes on earth, and who now enjoy the reward of
faith in heaven. We remember them not because by doing so we can add
to their glory; we remember them because we ourselves need reminding
that the call to holiness is for everyone.

November 7, 2010

THIRTY-SECOND SUNDAY
IN ORDINARY TIME

A reading from the holy Gospel
according to Luke   20:27, 34–38

Some Sadducees, those who deny that there is a
    resurrection,
    came forward.

Jesus said to them,
    "The children of this age marry and remarry;

but those who are deemed worthy to attain to
  the coming age
and to the resurrection of the dead
neither marry nor are given in marriage.
They can no longer die,
  for they are like angels;
and they are the children of God
because they are the ones who will rise.
That the dead will rise
  even Moses made known in the passage about
    the bush,
when he called out 'Lord,'
the God of Abraham, the God of Isaac,
  and the God of Jacob;
and he is not God of the dead, but of the living,
for to him all are alive."

The Gospel of the Lord.

Longer form: Luke 20:27–38

EXPLANATION OF THE READING

Throughout the month of November, which begins with All Saints and the Commemoration of the Faithful Departed, the Church prays for the dead. This Sunday's Gospel reading seems to be about marriage—but really it is about Resurrection. Then Sadducees deny the Resurrection, and they propose a hypothetical situation: a woman marries seven different brothers in turn, and is widowed seven times. Then Jesus is asked, Whose wife will she be in the Resurrection? His response sheds light on the nature of the Resurrection: We will not be as we were; instead, we become "like angels." The ties that bound us together on earth are dissolved; instead, we will discover new ways of being together, as "children of God."

November 14, 2010

THIRTY-THIRD SUNDAY IN ORDINARY TIME

A reading from the holy Gospel according to Luke

21:5–19

While some people were speaking about
  how the temple was adorned with costly stones
    and votive offerings,
  Jesus said, "All that you see here—
the days will come when there will not be left
a stone upon another stone that will not be
    thrown down."

Then they asked him,
  "Teacher, when will this happen?
And what sign will there be when all these things
    are about to happen?"
He answered,
"See that you not be deceived,
  for many will come in my name, saying,
  'I am he,' and 'The time has come.'
Do not follow them!
When you hear of wars and insurrections,
  do not be terrified; for such things must happen first,
  but it will not immediately be the end."

Then he said to them,
"Nation will rise against nation, and kingdom
     against kingdom.
There will be powerful earthquakes, famines,
     and plagues
   from place to place;
   and awesome sights and mighty signs will come
     from the sky.

"Before all this happens, however,
   they will seize and persecute you,
   they will hand you over to the synagogues and
     to prisons,
   and they will have you led before kings
     and governors
   because of my name.
It will lead to your giving testimony.
Remember, you are not to prepare your defense
     beforehand,
   for I myself shall give you a wisdom in speaking
   that all your adversaries will be powerless to resist
     or refute.
You will even be handed over by parents, brothers,
     relatives, and friends,
   and they will put some of you to death.
You will be hated by all because of my name,
   but not a hair on your head will be destroyed.
By your perseverance you will secure your lives."

The Gospel of the Lord.

EXPLANATION OF THE READING

Jesus urges his disciples not to put their trust in earthly things—no matter how stable and permanent they might seem. The temple, gloriously beautiful, richly adorned, the center of life and worship, seems like it will last forever, but Jesus foretells a time when it will be utterly destroyed. In the end, governments and kingdoms, too, will fall; even the face of the earth will be reshaped by earthquakes, and the fabric of families and relationships will be torn asunder as "parents, brothers, relatives, and friends" turn against each other. In God alone is the stability we seek.

November 21, 2010

SOLEMNITY OF OUR LORD JESUS CHRIST THE KING

A reading from the holy Gospel according to Luke 23:35–43

The rulers sneered at Jesus and said,
  "He saved others, let him save himself
  if he is the chosen one, the Christ of God."
Even the soldiers jeered at him.
As they approached to offer him wine they called
      out,
  "If you are King of the Jews, save yourself."
Above him there was an inscription that read,
  "This is the King of the Jews."

Now one of the criminals hanging there reviled Jesus,
      saying,
  "Are you not the Christ?
Save yourself and us."

The other, however, rebuking him, said in reply,
    "Have you no fear of God,
    for you are subject to the same condemnation?
And indeed, we have been condemned justly,
    for the sentence we received corresponds to our
        crimes,
    but this man has done nothing criminal."
Then he said,
    "Jesus, remember me when you come into your
        kingdom."
He replied to him,
    "Amen, I say to you,
    today you will be with me in Paradise."

The Gospel of the Lord.

EXPLANATION OF THE READING

The solemnity of Our Lord Jesus Christ the King is one of the newest on
the Church's calendar. It was instituted by Pope Pius XI in 1925. He hoped
that this proclamation of Christ as King of the universe would serve as
a corrective to the dangerous political ideas of his time—ideas that had
led to one devastating world war and would soon bring on another. Jesus
is a King like no other—a King who reigns from a cross, who has none
of the trappings of earthly power but who, choosing to empty himself,
leads us to paradise.

Patron Saints

The saints and blesseds are our companions in prayer on our journey with Christ. Here we provide you with a list of health concerns and the saints chosen to intercede on a sick person's behalf before God the Father.

AILMENTS	SAINT(S)
A	
abdominal pains	Agapitus; Charles Borromeo; Emerentiana; Erasmus; Liborius
abortion, protection against	Catherine of Sweden
abuse victims	Adelaide; Agostina Pietrantoni; Fabiola; John Baptist de la Salle; Germaine Cousin; Godelieve; Jeanne de Lestonnac; Jeanne Marie de Maille; Joaquina Vedruna de Mas; Laura Vicuna; Margaret the Barefooted; Maria Bagnesi; Monica; Pharaildis; Rita of Cascia
AIDS patients	Aloysius Gonzaga; Therese of Lisieux; Peregrine Lazios
alcoholism	John of God; Martin of Tours; Matthias the Apostle; Monica; Urban of Langres
angina sufferers	Swithbert
appendicitis	Erasmus (Elmo)
apoplexy, apoplexies, stroke, stroke victims	Andrew Avellino; Wolfgang
arm pain; pain in the arms	Amalburga

B

babies	The Holy Innocents; Maximus; Nicholas of Tolentino; Philip of Zell
bacterial disease and infection	Agrippina
barren women	Anthony of Padua; Felicity
barrenness, against	Agatha; Anne; Anthony of Padua; Casilda of Toledo; Felicity; Fiacre; Francis of Paola; Giles; Henry II; Margaret of Antioch; Medard; Philomena; Rita of Cascia; Theobald Roggeri
birth complications, against	Ulric
birth pains	Erasmus
blind people, blindness	Catald; Cosmas and Damian; Dunstan; Lawrence the Illuminator; Leodegarius; Lucy; Lutgardis; Odila; Parasceva; Raphael the Archangel; Thomas the Apostle
blood donors	Our Lady of the Thorns
bodily ills, illness, sickness	Alphais; Alphonsa of India; Angela Merici; Angela Truszkowska; Arthelais; Bathild; Bernadette of Lourdes; Camillus of Lellis; Catherine del Ricci; Catherine of Siena; Drogo; Edel Quinn; Elizabeth of the Trinity; Gerard of Villamagna; Germaine Cousin; Gorgonia; Hugh of Lincoln; Isabella of France; Jacinta Marto; John of God; Julia Billiart; Julia Falconieri; Juliana of Nicomedia; Louis IX; Louise de Marillac; Lydwina of Schiedam; Maria Bagnesi; Maria Gabriella; Maria Mazzarello; Marie Rose Durocher; Mary Ann de Paredes; Mary

Magdalen of Pazzi; Michael the
Archangel; Our Lady of Lourdes;
Paula Frassinetti; Peregrine Laziosi;
Philomena; Rafka Al-Rayes; Raphael;
Romula; Syncletica; Teresa of Avila;
Teresa Valse Pantellini; Terese of the
Andes; Therese of Lisieux

breast cancer	Agatha; Aldegundis; Giles; Peregrine
breast disease, against	Agatha
breastfeeding women	Giles
broken bones	Drogo; Stanislaus Kostka

C

cancer patients; against cancer	Aldegundis; Giles; James Salomone; Peregrine Laziosi
child abuse victims	Alodia; Germaine Cousin; Lufthild; Nunilo
childbirth	Erasmus; Gerard Majella; Leonard of Noblac; Lutgardis; Margaret (or Marina) of Antioch; Raymond Nonnatus
childhood diseases	Aldegundis; Pharaildis
childhood intestinal diseases	Erasmus
children, convulsive	Guy of Anderlecht; John the Baptist; Scholastica
children, death of	Alphonsa Hawthorne; Angela of Foligno; Clotilde; Conception Cabrera de Annida; Cyriacus of Iconium; Dorothy of Montau; Elizabeth of Hungary; Elizabeth Ann Seton; Felicity; Frances of Rome; Hedwig; Isidore the Farmer; Joaquina Vedruna de Mas; Julitta; Leopold the Good; Louis IX; Luchesius; Margaret of Scotland; Marguerite d'Youville; Matilda;

	Melania the Younger; Michelina; Nonna; Perpetua; Stephen of Hungary
children, sick	Beuno; Clement I; Hugh of Lincoln; Ubaldus Baldassini
children, stammering	Notkar Balbulus
colic	Agapitus; Charles Borromeo; Emerentiana; Erasmus; Liborius
contagious diseases	Robert Bellarmine; Sebastian
consumption	Pantaleon; Therese of Liseux
convulsions	John the Baptist; Willibrord
coughs, against	Blase; Quentin; Walburga
cramps, against	Cadoc of Llancarvan; Maurice; Pancras
cures from pain	Madron

D

deaf people, deafness	Cadoc of Llancarvan; Drogo; Francis de Sales; Meriadoc; Ouen
death	Michael the Archangel; Margaret (or Marina) of Antioch
death, happy	Joseph; Ulric
death, against sudden	Aldegundis; Andrew Avellino; Barbara; Christopher
disabled, handicapped	Alphais; Angela Merici; Gerald of Aurillac; Germaine Cousin; Giles; Henry II; Lutgardis; Margaret of Castello; Seraphina; Servatus; Servulus
drug abuse	Maximillian Kolbe
dying people, invoked by	Abel; Barbara; Benedict; Catherine of Alexandria; James the Lesser, Apostle; John of God; Joseph; Margaret (or

	Marina) of Antioch; Michael the Archangel; Nicholas of Tolentino; Sebastian
dysentary	Lucy of Syracuse; Polycarp

E

earache, against	Cornelius; Polycarp of Smyrna
epidemics	Godeberta; Lucy of Syracuse; Our Lady of Zapopan; Roch (Rocco)
epilepsy, epileptics	Alban of Mainz; Anthony the Abbot; Balthasar; Bibiana; Catald; Christopher; Cornelius; Dymphna; Genesius; Gerard of Lunel; Giles; Guy of Anderlecht; John Chrysostom; John the Baptist; Valentine; Vitus; Willibrord
ergotism, aginst	Anthony the Abbot
erysipelas	Anthony the Abbot; Benedict; Ida of Nivelles
expectant Mothers	Gerard Majella; Raymond Nonnatus
eyes, eye diseases, eye problems, sore eyes	Aloysius Gonzaga; Augustine of Hippo; Clare of Assisi; Cyriacus of Iconium; Erhard of Regensburg; Herve; Leodegarius; Lucy of Syracuse; Raphael the Archangel; Symphorian of Autun

F

fainting, faintness	Urban of Langres; Ursus of Ravenna; Valentine
fever, against	Abraham; Adalard; Amalberga; Andrew Abellon; Antoninus of Florence; Benedict; Castorus; Claudius; Cornelius; Dominic of Sora; Domitian of Huy; Four Crowned Martyrs; Genevieve;

	Gerebernus; Gertrude of Nivelles; Hugh of Cluny; Jodocus; Liborius; Mary of Oignies; Nicostratus; Peter the Apostle; Petronilla; Raymond Nonnatus; Severus of Avranches; Sigismund; Simpronian; Theobald Roggeri; Ulric; Winnoc
fistula	Fiacre
frenzy, against	Denis; Peter the Apostle; Ulric
foot problems; feet problems	Peter the Apostle; Servatus

G

gall stones	Benedict; Drogo; Florentius of Strasburg; Liborius
goiter	Blase
gout, against; gout sufferers	Andrew the Apostle; Coloman; Gerebernus; Gregory the Great; Killian; Maurice; Maurus; Totman

H

hangovers	Bibiana
head injuries	John Licci
headaches	Acacius; Anastasius the Persian; Bibiana; Denis; Dionysius the Aeropagite; Gerard of Lunel; Gereon; Pancras; Stephen the Martyr; Teresa of Avila; William Firmatus
health	Infant Jesus of Prague
healthy throats	Andrew the Apostle; Blase; Etheldreda; Godelieve; Ignatius of Antioch; Lucy of Syracuse; Swithbert
heart patients	John of God
hemorrhage	Lucy

hemorrhoid, piles	Fiacre
hernia	Alban of Mainz; Condrad Piacenzai; Cosmas and Damian; Drogo; Gummarus
herpes	George
hoarseness, against	Bernadine of Sienna; Maurus
hydrophobia (rabies)	Dominic de Silos; Guy of Anderlecht; Hubert of Liege; Otto of Bamberg; Sithney; Walburga

I

infertility, against	Agatha; Anne; Anthony of Padua; Casilda of Toledo; Felicity; Fiacre; Francis of Paola; Giles; Henry II; Margaret of Antioch; Medard; Philomena; Rita of Cascia; Theobald Roggeri
inflammatory disease	Benedict
intestinal diseases, against	Brice; Charles Borromeo; Emerentiana; Erasmus; Timonthy; Wolfgang
invalids, homebound	Roch (Rocco)

J

jauntice	Odilo

K

kidney disease, against	Benedict; Drogo; Margaret (or Marina) of Antioch; Ursus of Ravenna
kidney stones; gravel	Alban of Mainz
knee diseases or trouble	Roch (Rocco)

L

lame, the	Giles
leg diseases, leg trouble	Servatus

lepers, leprosy	George; Giles; Lazarus; Vincent de Paul
long life	Peter the Apostle
lumbago	Lawrence

M

mental illness	Benedict Joseph Labre; Bibiana; Christina the Astonishing; Drogo; Dymphna; Eustochium of Padua; Fillan; Giles; Job; Margaret of Cortona; Maria Fortunata Viti; Medard; Michelina; Osmund; Raphaela; Romanus of Condat; Veran
migraine	Gereon; Severus of Avranches; Ulbadus Baldassini
milk, loss of by nursing women	Margaret of Antioch
miscarriage, against	Catherine of Sienna; Catherine of Sweden; Eulalia
miscarriage prevention	Catherine of Sweden
muteness	Drogo

N

near sightedness, short sightedness	Clarus; Abbot
nerve or neurological disease, against	Bartholomew the Apostle; Dymphna
nursing mothers	Concordia; Martina

O

obsession	Quirinus

P

pain relief	Madron
paralysis	Catald; Osmund; Wolfgang

physical spouse abuse, against; victims of spouse abuse, against	Rita of Cascia
plague, against	Adrian of Nicomedia; Catald; Colman of Stockerau; Cuthbert; Edmund of East Anglia; Erhard of Regensburg; Francis of Paola; Francis Xavier; George; Genevieve; Gregory the Great; Macarius of Antioch; Roch (Rocco); Sebastian; Valentine; Walburga
poison sufferers	Benedict; Abbot; John the Apostles; Pirmin
pregnant women, pregnancy	Anne; Anthony of Padua; Elizabeth; Gerard Majella; Joseph; Margaret (or Marina) of Antioch; Raymond Nonnatus; Ulric

R

rape victims	Agatha; Agnes of Rome; Antona Messina; Dymphna; Joan of Arc; Maria Goretti; Pierina Morosini; Potamiaena; Solange; Zita
rheumatism, arthritis	Alphonus Maria de Liguori; Coloman; James the Greater; Killian; Servatus; Totnan
respiratory problems	Bernadine of Sienna
ruptures, against	Drogo; Florentius of Strasburg; Osmund

S

scrofulous diseases	Balbina; Marculf; Mark the Evangelist
skin disease	Anthony the Abbot; George; Marculf; Peregrine Laziosi; Roch (Rocco)
skin rashes	Anthony the Abbot; George; Marculf; Peregrine Laziosi; Roch (Rocco)

sleepwalkers, sleepwalking	Dymphna
smallpox	Matthias
snakebite victims	Hilary; Paul
spasms	John the Baptist
sterility, against	Agatha; Anne; Anthony of Padua; Casilda of Toledo; Felicity; Fiacre; Francis of Paola; Giles; Henry II; Margaret of Antioch; Medard; Philomena; Rita of Cascia; Theobald Roggeri
stillborn children	Edmund
stomach disease, stomach trouble	Brice; Charles Borromeo; Erasmus; Timothy; Wolfgang
stroke	Andrew Avellino; Wolfgang
struma	Balbina; Marculf; Mark the Evangelist
surgery patients	Infant of Prague
syphilis	Fiacre; George; Symphoroian of Autun

T

throat diseases, against	Andrew the Apostle; Blaise; Etheldreda; Godelieve; Ignatius of Antioch; Lucy of Syracuse; Swithbert
toothaches	Apollonia; Chirstopher; Elizabeth of Hungary; Ida of Nivelles; Kea; Medard; Osmund
tuberculosis	Pantaleon; Theresa of Liseaux
twitching, against	Bartholomew the Apostle; Cornelius
typhus, against; against typhoid	Adelard

u

ulcers, against	Charles Borromeo; Job

V

venereal disease	Fiacre
verbal spousal abuse	Anne Marie Taigi; Godelieve; Monica
vertigo, against	Ulric

W

whooping cough, against	Blaise; Winoc
women in labor	Anne; Erasmus; John of Bridlington; Margaret (or Marina) of Antioch; Margaret of Fontana; Mary of Oignies
women who wish to be mothers	Andrew the Apostle
wounds	Aldegundis; Marciana; Rita of Cascia